S0-AGM-586

THE WAR AT SIXTEEN

**By the same author
from the same publishers**

The Distant Lands
(a novel of the antebellum South)

Paris
(essays — bilingual)

South
(a play)

The Apprentice Writer
(essays)

The Green Paradise
(Autobiography Vol. I, 1900–1916)

JULIAN GREEN

THE WAR AT
SIXTEEN

Autobiography
Volume II (1916–1919)

Translated by
Euan Cameron

Marion Boyars
New York · London

Published in the
United States and Great Britain in 1993
by Marion Boyars Publishers
237 East 39th Street, New York, N.Y. 10016
24 Lacy Road, London, SW15 1NL
Distributed in Australia and New Zealand by
Peribo Pty Ltd, 26 Tepko Road, Terrey Hills, NSW 2084
Previously published in France under the title
Mille Chemins Ouverts in 1984 by Editions du Seuil
© Editions du Seuil 1984
© This translation Euan Cameron 1993

All rights reserved.
No part of this publication may be reproduced, stored in a retrieval system or
transmitted in any form or by any means, electronic, mechanical, photocopying,
recording or otherwise except brief extracts for the purposes of review, without
prior written permission of the publishers.

Any paperback edition of this book whether published simultaneously with or
subsequent to, the casebound edition is sold subject to the condition that it shall
not by way of trade, be lent, resold, hired out or otherwise disposed of without
the publishers' consent, in any form of binding or cover other than that in which
it was published.

The rights of Julian Green and Euan Cameron to be identified as authors of this
work have been asserted by them in accordance with the Copyright, Designs and
Patents Act 1988.

Library of Congress Cataloging-in-Publication-Data
Green, Julian, 1900–
    [Mille chemins ouverts. English]
    The war at sixteen: autobiography/Julian Green.
    Contents: v. 2. 1916–1919.
        1. Green, Julian, 1900–   —Biography—Youth.   2. Authors,
            French—20th century—Biography.   3. Authors,
American—20th
                                    century—Biography.   4. World Wa
, 1914–1918—Personal narratives,
    French.   I. Title.
    PQ2613.R3Z477   1993
    843'.912—dc20
    [B]   93–656
British Library Cataloguing in Publication Data Green, Julian
    War at Sixteen: Autobiography. – Vol. 2:
    1916–19
    I. Title   II. Cameron, Euan
    843.912
            ISBN 0–7145–2969–9 Cloth

Typeset in 11/13 Baskerville and Bodoni by
Ann Buchan (Typesetters), Middx.

Printed in Great Britain by Loader Jackson, Arlesey.

About the Author

Born in 1900 of American parents living in Paris, Julian Green has spent most of his extraordinary literary career there, writing now in French for a wide and enthusiastic readership. He has published over sixty books in France: novels, essays, plays, a four-volume autobiography (of which this is the second), and, so far, fourteen volumes of his Journal. Initially writing in English, he published a number of celebrated books in England and the United States before writing almost exclusively in French.

As an American, Julian Green is the only foreign member of the Académie Française. He is also a member of the American Academy of Arts and Letters, winner of the Harper Prize, the Prix Marcel Proust, the Prix France-Amérique, the Prix Cavour and numerous other international awards. In 1993 he was presented with the Benson Medal by the Royal Society of Literature in London. He is one of the few living authors to have their collected works published in the prestigious Gallimard Pléiade series.

Julian Green's epic novel of the antebellum South *The Distant Lands* was published in 1991, simultaneously with his play *South* which is set on the eve of the Civil War. The sequel to *The Distant Lands*, set during the Civil War, will be published in 1994.

His book of essays about Paris with a selection of the author's own photographs of his favourite city is available from the same publishers. His early writings in English under the title *The Apprentice Writer* was published in 1993.

Julian Green lives in Paris.

Introduction

Writing from New York during World War II, in the foreword to *Memories of Happy Days*, one of the few books he ever wrote in English, Julian Green paid affectionate tribute to the France that he loved. The first pages of that book were written within days of his arrival in America, shocked and heavy-hearted at the humiliation the French nation was enduring. 'It is impossible that she will disappear', he wrote, 'but if she did, a great many reasons for being attached to this life would disappear with her. She has given us more than we know, she has made this world richer and more beautiful for millions of men and women; if she ever went, we might not cease to live, but we should be poorer and something in us would die.' For Green, then a man of forty years of age, it was the second time that his world had collapsed into the nightmare of war.

As he left the shores of France behind him in 1940, by then a respected and successful novelist, Julian Green's thoughts must surely have returned to that earlier, even bloodier, Great War which he had witnessed directly, and to the sense of desolation he experienced when he had been obliged to leave the land of his birth for the first time. That was in 1919; and Europe, after four years that had irrevocably altered the world in which he had grown up, was at peace at last. He was nineteen and on his way to enrol as a student at the University of Virginia. It was not only the war that was finally over; so too was an adolescence that had been full of more than its normal share of pain, sorrow and drama.

American, but born and brought up in Paris, Julian

Green was the youngest in a family of eight children. He was fourteen when he lost his mother. A strikingly beautiful woman, and a devout Protestant who was fiercely proud of her Southern blood (she came from Savannah, Georgia), she and her son's memories of her have been the crucial and abiding influences on Green's life and work. It was shortly after this that Green decided to become a convert to Catholicism, never realizing that his father had secretly taken the same step only months before. The anguish of his mother's death, his subsequent spiritual awakening and his earliest childhood memories are described with unusual frankness in Green's first autobiographical book, *Partir avant le Jour* (translated as *The Green Paradise* — Marion Boyars, 1992).

When he was only sixteen, Green's world was to turn over again. In 1917, encouraged by his patriotic father to 'do something' for the war effort, Julian was sent to the front line as an ambulance driver in the American Field Service. He was posted to the Argonne forest in North-Eastern France where, in the evenings, shortly after his arrival, he heard the low rumble of battle reverberating from the furnace of nearby Verdun. It was here, too, that the horror he felt at the sight of a young dead soldier made him a pacifist for life.

Later, when it was discovered that he was actually too young to be at the war, Green was sent home to Paris; but he soon managed to enlist in the American Red Cross and set off to serve as an ambulance driver once more, this time on the Italian front, north of Venice. Although no two writers could have less in common, it is strange to reflect that at the same time, not very far away, another young American, who was only one year older than Green and also an ambulance driver — a man who also came to love France, though for rather different reasons — Lieutenant

Ernest Hemingway, was living through some of the experiences he later put to fictional use in *A Farewell to Arms*.

In the summer of 1918, Green enroled in the École d'Artillerie at Fontainebleau, and it was as an officer-cadet in the French Army that he saw out the last months of the war. After the Armistice, he accompanied his regiment to the Rhineland on occupation duty and there he remained until he was demobilized in 1919.

It is the last two years of the First World War and its immediate aftermath that form the period covered by *The War at Sixteen*. We leave him on board ship, missing Paris badly, with the New World beckoning and the New York skyline glimpsed on the horizon. Three years of student life in the South (the subject of his third volume of autobiography, *Terre Lointaine*) lay ahead of him.

Yet if the devastation that ravaged Europe forms the backdrop to *The War at Sixteen*, it is not really the subject of the book. War to a spirit such as Green's is terrible and unacceptable, but it is only to be expected as the result of man's folly and lack of faith. As in his marvellous *Journal* (a diary begun in 1926 which has now reached Volume 15 and which must certainly be the longest record of a writer's life and times in modern literature) worldly events are observed and commented upon, but they are of little consequence compared to a man's spiritual, artistic and emotional development.

It was only when he reached the University of Virginia that Green became fully aware of his true sexual nature, yet the war years were also an important period of growing sexual awareness for him, and his brief *éducations sentimentales* with Lola in Genoa and the 'blond cadet' in Oberlinxweiler are delightfully comic and tender interludes by comparison with the agonies of guilt and spiritual torment

— the 'crucifixion of the flesh' — that future liaisons were to bring.

Green is equally frank about his religious preoccupations. Well schooled in the Bible by his Episcopalian mother, he seems to have been a Catholic by conviction while remaining a Protestant in his love of literal truth. The fervour induced in him by his Jesuit mentor persuaded him that he was destined for the religious life, and it was only a quirk of fate that prevented him from entering the monastery of Quarr Abbey on the Isle of Wight to become a Benedictine novice.

'*Mes livres sont des livres de prisonnier qui rêve de liberté. . .*', he wrote in *Journal V*, and throughout Green's work we have a certain image of man chained unwillingly to his fleshly desires while simultaneously yearning for liberation. However, we should remember that in these autobiographical books it is an older, wiser Green — he was sixty-four when he wrote *The War at Sixteen* — who is holding a mirror to the boy and young man he had been, and trying to grasp that 'gossamer thread that passes through my life from birth to death, the one that guides, binds, explains'.

Many writers have sought to look back at their past and to recreate and confront their younger selves, but few have ever done so with quite as much openness and with such scrupulous honesty as Julian Green does in these four volumes of autobiography. Perfectionist and lover of truth that he is, Green would accept nothing less; it would be no more than his duty to his maker, to his readers, and to himself.

Euan Cameron
London, June 1993

The mysterious path leads
towards what is innermost.
                    Novalis

'Tomorrow we're leaving for the front!' The rumour had spread throughout the day only to be denied the next morning. Our hearts were beating anxiously for we had not the vaguest idea what the front could be, and we could not know that twenty letters from twenty young American boys announcing the news to their families had been suppressed by the censor. Our ambulances waited patiently along Triaucourt's main street and gradually the tedium of waiting wore down our spirits.

These were vital days in my life. I had left my classmates in Rhetoric and now found that I was surrounded by a new group of boys hardly older than myself but very different. They did not speak the same language. They spoke freely of their Parisian exploits, or about their home towns which they still missed, but I was not interested in the girls they boasted about and I knew very little about the country whose charms and, particularly, whose comforts they spoke of so highly. In fact they were from the North or the West and I was the only one who could call myself a Southerner. What is more, I was the only Catholic. When they discovered, after cross-questioning me, that I was born in Paris, the city of pleasure and the capital of sinfulness, but had never set foot in the United States, their questions increased, although I never understood their curiosity, for what struck them as strange was entirely normal to me.

Most of the boys came from the better-known universities and spoke correctly even if it was not an accent that I was used to, and because they were in uniform and desperately needed to think of themselves as soldiers, they felt obliged to swear. Blasphemy was something that horrified me then and has continued to do so to this day. There was one boy, however, who was different and who was training for the Presbyterian ministry. Tall and thin, with a very serious expression, his name was Phinney. One rainy day he found me in my ambulance reading the Bible (the Crampon translation). The marvellous aroma of the cigarette he was smoking transported me to another world in which I seemed to see people drinking champagne.

'What the devil. . .', I wondered vaguely.

'What are you reading, Green?'

'The Holy Bible.'

'In French?'

'Yes, in French.'

'Catholic, are you?'

With each answer I gave, I made sure this heretic noticed the little aluminium medal that I wore on my wrist and on which I had carved with my penknife the words 'Julian Green, Roman Catholic'. We had all been given one of these medals at the rue Raynouard before leaving Paris and it had been explained to us that should we be killed they would be needed for identification. 'Should we be killed. . .' What an absurd thought! It was inconceivable that I should be killed, but I nevertheless wanted everyone to know that I was a Catholic. Phinney smiled indulgently. In fifteen minutes he had discovered all that he needed to know; that is to say that I was a member of the faith, that I wished to become a priest and, in a roundabout way, that I was a virgin. He didn't mention that again. Nobody did, for they all discovered the truth eventually. A Parisian who had never touched a woman — you could hardly believe it! What about Montmartre and the renowned corruptness of that modern Babylon? I looked at them with astonishment. 'It's not possible,' one of them said. 'Boy, you don't know what's good for you.' Phinney elbowed him violently and he shut up.

These things come back to me after so many years with such acuteness that I cannot recall them without a certain sadness. How could I not see that I was worth so much more then?

I had forgotten my shameful experiences in Genoa.* All my religious impulses returned to me, the surging fervour, the hatred of evil, by which I mean impurity. It seemed to me that in one stroke this contact with Protestantism brought it all back to me. I wanted to be martyred for the faith. My imagination soared wildly, but nobody had the slightest wish to hang, draw or quarter me. On the contrary, everyone showed a disarming friendship and made allowances for everything: the South, the Roman Catholic church, my appalling ignorance of the facts of life, and they regarded me rather as a lost child among men, in an ambulance service that had no need of me. I seldom spoke, but I replied to all their questions with a frankness which, as I was well aware, provoked disbelief: I had been a Catholic for one year having abjured Luther's heresy; I belonged to the South in every imaginable way and had not a drop of Northern blood in my veins, and as for the war of Secession, we ought to have won it because our generals were just as good as yours and our troops just as brave, but you had more men.

* See *The Green Paradise*, Volume I of Julian Green's autobiography.

One day a Jewish comrade took me to one side. He was called Heiden.

'Who told you all that about the war?'

'My mother.'

'She shouldn't have. We have to forget it.'

'We'll never forget. It's not true that we were defeated because of slavery. We were right.'

'We've got to forget. We're all Americans.'

'Yes, but we were right and we should have won.'

Heiden nodded. 'One day you must come to our home. Everything that is good on earth is there.'

I listened in silence, somewhat incredulously, but as long as he didn't speak about the War, I was happy.

At Triaucourt I loved God. I had the sense of being almost huddled against him. If these words appear meaningless, it is because I am attempting to speak of things which are perhaps inexplicable. I don't remember going to Mass, probably because the church was in the out of bounds sector, but as we were allowed to do as we pleased while we waited for orders which never came, I would wander in a small field and climb the lower branches of a fine tree. Seated in my hard chair up there, I would spend long periods sunk in reflection. The church could not have been far away, for on Sundays I distinctly heard the chant of Vespers. I shall never forget one summer afternoon hearing the words of the *Dixit Dominus* out of a brilliant blue sky. '. . .*sede a dextris meis*. . .'. There was such reassurance and happiness in those words and that music that I had the feeling I was being transported out of this world. I had in my hands a small pocket missal which my father had given me on the day I left home and my heart beat with a mysterious joy. Was it a truly Christian joy? I don't know. I was simply ecstatically happy to be alive and it was as if something was lifting me up in the way a powerful hand might pick up a kitten. The image may seem bizarre, nevertheless it expresses what I want to say. I had never been drunk, yet that must be a similar sensation.

A few days later we left Triaucourt for a village whose name I have forgotten. We were billeted in a large farmhouse where we got very bored waiting for our orders. Waiting: it seems to me that the word sums up an entire aspect of wars throughout history, for waiting can also be a form of torture. I remember being made to drive my ambulance one way, then another, between two rows of posts, from morning to night, just as we we did at Moulin-de-Meaux;* unaccomplished though I was, I eventually learned to drive.

I have sometimes wondered why we were sent there when our ultimate destination was Clermont-en-Argonne. I have the impression that no one knew exactly what to do with us, which is why we were sent here and there in the hope that an idea would occur to someone. In any case, towards the end of August we found ourselves in a large and attractive house belonging to a notary from Clermont. I never saw the notary and the house was empty. Our dormitory on the first floor looked out over a magnificent terrace planted with trees and nothing could have been more peaceful than the view we had from the large windows: beyond the valley there were wooded hills which turned blue in the evening light. Our commanding officer told us we were no longer very far from the front, although here we were hardly aware of the reality of war.

* See *The Green Paradise*

However, there were a number of French soldiers in their sky-blue uniforms who had been attached to our section and one would have had to be blind not to notice that this posting was a godsend for them. One of them in particular remains in my memory because of something he said to me. He was a large boy with gentle eyes who had worked in a factory before the war. He spoke about women in an unconstrained way to some of my comrades, telling them stories that I found horrifying. I was convinced that he did not believe in God. One day when I was reading my Bible in a corner of the dining-room, he came and sat down close to me and asked me politely if he could 'see the beautiful book'. Zealously, I put it in front of his nose but he looked disappointed as he turned the pages. 'There are no pictures', he said with a smile. I was expecting some sort of blasphemy and had already prepared my response. His remark took me by surprise and I did not say a word, something for which I reproached myself afterwards, for I reasoned that I should have explained my beliefs, but a mixture of shame and human respect made me keep silent. I experienced a sort of pain, as if I had committed a real sin, and it was as if I had denied Christ in the way that Peter did with the servant-girl. Once I was sure there was no one there a need for solitude made me go up to the dormitory.

We had parked our ambulances under the trees of the terrace so as to camouflage them from the enemy, but in the end they must have been discovered for one day German planes were seen above Clermont. It was shortly before lunch and I was alone reading in the dormitory. I heard someone call out, 'Everyone to the cellar', and I went to look out of the window. It was then that my conduct became inexplicable. 'Everyone to the cellar', seemed incomprehensible. If it was an order it could not apply to me. Obedient though I was by nature, the idea of going down to the cellar was inconceivable. If I did go down it would mean I no longer believed in God, since I knew he would protect me and that nothing could happen to me. I had such a strong sense of security up there alone in the dormitory that to leave it would have been to defy Heaven. Muffled explosions could be heard some way away from the house. I knelt down, said a prayer and sat down on my bed. About ten minutes later, the voices of my comrades on the terrace told me that the danger had passed and I went downstairs.

No one questioned me. No one took any notice of me. I realized that something had happened and that everyone was upset. A boy from Chicago had had a nervous breakdown during the alert and it had been necessary to isolate him in a deeper cellar. 'He was frightened', someone murmured. 'We can't have him here.' That day the commanding officer came towards me, twisting the ends of his little moustache, and with a fierce expression said, 'You must do something for me. You will take so-and-so to the station in your ambulance. After that, you will return here.'

I hardly knew the so-and-so in question. Apparently he smoked too much. He was a small, dark man with restless eyes and a blue chin. His friends bade him good-bye rather awkwardly and he climbed up next to me in the ambulance. He did not reply when I spoke to him and he seemed to be on the point of bursting into tears. I don't know whether there was a train or a lorry at the station for I only stayed with him a moment. He avoided my look and I started to say anything that came to my mind; pointless and inopportune remarks, I expect, for life is cruel and malicious, but I had been ashamed of the way they had said good-bye to him. I ought to have embraced him in front of the soldiers who were there, but I was shy. When the moment came, I smiled and shook his hand, but that was as far as my compassion went.

When I returned to the house I found our boss Mr Ware (the French called him Mistaire Ouaire) sitting at the end of a table in the refectory. Nearly all my colleagues were there too, but they were at the back of the room, and I had the feeling he had just been speaking to them. He asked me if I had taken so-and-so to the station and when I said yes he gave me a tigerish smile and in rather studied English he uttered the following words which I have never forgotten: 'Allow me to offer you my sincere congratulations'.

At that moment a sentence came to my mind which seemed to dance before my eyes in flashing letters while an inner voice urged me, 'Say it! Tell the man!' I had the time. Mr Ware was expecting me to say something. 'I have done nothing to deserve your congratulations.' I did not say that. The sentence stuck in my throat because I was frightened. Suddenly it dawned on me: I had no fear of the German Taube bombs for I was sure that nothing in the world could harm me, but I was frightened of men, frightened of arousing their anger and frightened of Mr Ware. Without replying I saluted him and walked towards my colleagues in silence. For a second or two no one moved, then the dry voice of Mr Ware broke out: 'Very well. You are all dismissed'.

I was greatly disturbed by the notion that I had been inwardly afraid in front of another man while God, it seemed to me, had told me to speak out bravely. Outwardly, nothing had changed. In others' eyes I was the same rather timid, helpless boy who, ever so slightly, had to be discreetly supervised, yet something had happened within me. Once more I had the feeling that I had betrayed

Christ, because Christ was with the boy I had taken to the station. That troubled me and, strange though it may seem, troubles me still when I think about it. No one spoke any more about the boy who had returned home in disgrace. His ambulance was put aside. In a very short time it would be badly needed.

On alternate days we were sent to the first-aid posts situated just behind the front line. There we spent the night and the next day waiting, as the need arose, to take any wounded to the nearest hospital. Generally, there were very few, for our sector was a relatively quiet one. When it was my turn to be sent to the front I could hardly control my impatience. I imagined that at last we would see the trenches which I had heard so much about for so long and which I would be able to describe to my father when I wrote. But nothing like that happened.

There were two of us to an ambulance. One drove on the way there, the other on the way back. On this occasion I was chosen to go with a boy who I shall call Earle. We had never spoken to each other before, not because I did not want to, but because I was nervous. He had a handsome face and such a very bored look that even I could not fail to know what it meant. Like everyone else, I knew that all Earle ever thought about were the pretty girls in Paris. He had the reputation for being debauched and an irresistible seducer, which created an aura of glory about him and commanded respect. Personally, I didn't know what to think of him. Surely, he was a sinner bound for damnation. In any case, every time I looked at him I was reminded of Bocaccio's stories and the other books in the collection of erotic drawings and engravings by Italian masters that I had seen in Mr Kreyer's library in Genoa.* But it would be hypocritical if I did not admit that I found the prospect rather appealing. There was something evil and seductive about him, and I cannot deny that I was unaware of his strange charm. Perhaps he will talk to me about Paris, I thought to myself. In which case I shan't listen; but perhaps he will talk about it all the same.

He was to drive on the outward journey. When I sat down next to him and he saw that his companion was to be the baby of the section, or to be more honest, its virgin, he gave me a look which is hard to describe but which clearly said, 'That's all I need'.

We left Clermont and drove in silence through the deserted villages and the woods until, towards the end of the afternoon, we entered one of the most beautiful forests imaginable. The road was appalling and we bumped along. Without speaking, I observed my companion's sullen face under the rim of his blue helmet, for we wore helmets just like the soldiers. His teeth clenched, Earle kept his eyes fixed firmly ahead of him. I only retain a confused picture of the first-aid post. All I remember is that there were fairly large numbers of soldiers tramping over duck-boards in between enormous trees. There was mud everywhere and shell-craters all over the place, but in spite of this it still had a magical beauty. I was only sorry that there were so many trees which had been split in two as if by an axe. A junior officer who had come to meet us explained that occasionally shells fell and if they came when we were outside we should throw ourselves flat on our stomachs. He also showed us the shelter where we were to spend the night. It was a sort of dug-out with two wooden pillars which held up the ceiling and two beds with mattresses. A lamp had been

* See *The Green Paradise*

placed on the ground between the beds.

After dinner we went to bed. I had taken out my Crampon Bible from my haversack and tried to read, but it was impossible. The lamp was dim and there was no table to put it on. Just then some demon prompted me to speak to Earle who had just got into bed.

'Hey, Earle, do you like Paris?'

A grunt was his only reply.

I persisted. 'You know, I was born in Paris and I've actually spent all my life there.'

'Oh, kid, be quiet. Go to sleep.'

I bit my lips. 'If we want to sleep we'll have to put out the light.'

'Oh, really!'

'Why not?'

'You'll see soon enough. Sleep!'

Slipping under my rug, I pulled it up under my left ear and began to say my prayers, for I could not bring myself to say them on my knees in front of Earle. I fell asleep almost immediately but a moment later there was a loud crash and I heard Earle swearing horribly.

'That's it,' he shouted. 'The bastards have knocked over the lamp. What a country!'

I opened my eyes. It was completely dark. At the same time I was aware of a scurrying and a sound of squeaking around my bed. I must have fallen asleep again, but in the early morning I was awoken by the same noise and in the dawn light which shone through the crack under the door, I noticed four or five rats roughly the size of small dogs. I realized that the reason the lamp had been left lit was to keep them at bay, but whoever had put it there did not know the rats of the Argonne forest. They had knocked over our lamp with total disdain! I hurriedly covered my head with the blanket and went back to sleep.

Little happened during the next day and we returned to Clermont.

Some letters arrived from Paris. One from my father, full of advice ('make sure you are obedient'), and one from my poor sister Retta who had just had an operation but was still able to give me all the family news in a suitably witty manner that cheered me up. In a post-script she added the following sentence which puzzled me: 'I am absolutely certain that you will be brave.' She did not know, as I did, that nothing affected me and that I could not even begin to imagine a physical fear such as that of the boy who had broken down in the cellar. My fear was of a different kind. I had a fear of God, which accounted for the sense of panic that sin inspired in me, and I also had a fear of men. Why? Because it seemed to me that these men represented God's will: either they had to be obeyed, or, on the other hand, they had to be refuted and stopped. That's where my problems started, since I would have preferred to throw myself on them and fight them with all my strength rather than argue with them. The violence in my character was such that the words I ought to have spoken stuck in my throat and, no longer in command of myself, I was frightened of what I might actually say. I did not have sufficient presence of mind politely to make wounding or telling remarks. I felt inferior even to those that my pride told me were beneath me. They knew how to reply. I did not. I was frightened of them and of myself. A murderer sleeps within us. It was he whom I feared. I cannot explain my gentleness any other way. I swallowed my anger. The fury which so often boiled up in me had to do with a sexual craving which would only manifest itself much later . . . but

I've strayed far from the subject of the letters I received. There were some from Father Crété too, full of concern, I am sure, but illegible. The words 'Do you take Communion?' stood out, however. But I did not go to Communion. If there was a chaplain, I never saw him. Where we were, the churches were roofless and empty. Finally, there was a note from Frédéric, one of the friends I had so admired at the lycée, who expressed his patriotic feelings in strong handwriting. I read those lines again and again. He called me Julian.

One evening after dinner, the Jewish boy, Heiden, took me to one side and asked me to follow him onto the terrace. It was a beautiful night, the smells of summer were still in the air, and I was thinking what an excellent idea my friend had had when he suddenly said,

'Listen.'

We kept still for a moment.

'A storm,' I muttered.

'No. If it were thunder the noise would stop occasionally. This noise is constant.'

It was actually a low, distant, rumbling sound that never stopped.

'It's Verdun,' said Heiden.

I shuddered at the mention of this sinister yet fascinating name. There, I knew I really would have been frightened. There, my intestines would certainly have turned to liquid like those of King David in the Psalms. Verdun was a hell, and the noise I heard in the distance was the ghastly rattle of death, the vast black hole where the armies of two nations were being swallowed up. I could not utter a word and after a while we returned. Who were the brave on this earth? Those men who were frightened yet appeared not to be. If only this noise would stop just for an hour . . . but it continued for several days.

One evening when we were at Islettes (which was the name of a particular part of the forest), shells started to fall all around us. I was outside with my companion and I threw myself flat on the ground among the dead leaves each time I heard the warning sound. I had learned to distinguish between the whine of the 150 mm type of shell and the whistle of another type which we were told was even deadlier. In any case, we lost no time in getting back to our shelter and we were already asleep when a soldier came to tell us to report to another first-aid post to collect a wounded man. The shelling had almost stopped and I ran to the place where we had left our ambulance.

That morning I had washed the ambulance thoroughly, getting rid of all the mud that had made it look rather a mess. With a small electric lamp in my hand, I searched for it among the trees.

'Where is she?' I called out to my companion.

'I don't know. Some one must have taken it.'

Suddenly he let out a yell and, pointing to the trees, revealed all that was left of our vehicle. Hit by a shell, it had simply burst into fragments which were now lodged haphazardly among the branches around us.

'But I'd only just washed her', I groaned (as if that were a reason).

My companion (this time it was not Earle) was a sensible, reserved, and I think rather shy boy. For him there was no point in wondering what had happened. We had to get back to our dug-out at all cost, and I would have agreed with him had I not noticed another ambulance of the same type as ours a little further away. Afraid of disobeying an order, it occurred to me to take this one instead to the place where we were supposed to be.

'You drive,' I said to my companion.

A surprise awaited us on the road. The shells, which had fallen almost everywhere, had made craters along our path and from time to time we heard the sound of bombs about to explode some distance away from us. In my view there was scarcely any danger but my friend was clearly very worried and I admired him, for in spite of his anxiety, he quickly came round to my way of thinking. We decided that I would proceed on foot and would blow a whistle to tell him where there were shell holes. Avoiding them was not always easy and we took at least fifteen minutes before reaching a more or less normal road.

Because of my notion that God's personal protection would allow nothing to harm me, I was not affected at all by any of this. Today I realise the enormity of my presumption. I really believed that God would deliver me from all evil and that I was in no more danger at Argonne than I would have been at Passy, where we lived in Paris. Perhaps the word presumption is too strong. This trust was the basis of my religion and I owed it to my mother and to the literal interpretation she had given to Psalm 23 which she had made me learn by heart. God, I thought, had given me his word and I relied on it. I didn't ask myself why others were being killed and wounded. Did God not protect them?

In any case, I could not be touched, even literally. It shames me to write that if anybody accidentally brushed against me I pulled away with a sort of revulsion. The catechism's use of the word 'touch' was probably responsible for this morbid peculiarity. I could never even sit down at a place that someone else had just left because the heat that his body left behind made me feel uneasy.

My friend, whose poor pale face betrayed his fear, was very different from me and much more human. He had done his duty well in spite of being frightened. I had done mine like a sleepwalker or a madman. . . Of the two of us, he was the one who showed real courage. I have forgotten his name. I have forgotten the condition of the wounded man we came to collect or where we took him. I can only recall the things I have just mentioned.

I remember that once when I was sitting in the sun outside the notary's house, four or five of my colleagues came up and began to cross-question me, partly in order to tease me, for my replies appeared to astonish them and they must have wondered whether I was mad, stupid or intelligent, all three hypotheses being possible. I didn't mind this interrogation, for it was not malicious, but once or twice I felt at a loss for words. Eventually one of the boys said to me with a dirty grin:

'You should go to bed with someone. It would do you good.'

The devil again, I thought, looking at him. But what ought I to say? I kept silent.

'You've shocked him', someone else said. 'He doesn't even know what you're talking about.'

Remembering everything that I had read in Mr Kreyer's library in Genoa, I wanted to tell them that I was fully informed on these matters, but I was not sure where such a discussion might lead and so I kept quiet, not without a certain awkwardness for I felt vaguely hypocritical and, deep down, I did want to hear about these things. Despite everything, I was frightened of sin.

I am not sure how the conversation took on a religious slant but I then became much more talkative.

'Who told you there is a Purgatory? Your Church? The Pope?'

I could feel my heart thumping. 'If you read your Bible in a full translation, you'll find Purgatory mentioned.'

'Oh? And whereabouts?'

'In the Book of Maccabees where the mother of Maccabees prays for the soul of her son who has been killed in battle.'

'What's the Book of Maccabees?'

'Leave him alone,' said another boy. 'You'll never convince him.'

They continued to joke and tease me before going away. 'In any case,' one of them said, 'if ever you become a bishop you'll look marvellous in purple.'

While waiting to turn purple I blushed, because I thought of all my own sins of the flesh and I wished I could have told these men that I was not quite as innocent as they might imagine.

When I was alone, Phinney came up and said, 'I see you read the Bible regularly. Do you remember the place where the Lord says to his disciples, "You are the salt of the earth." '?

'Perfectly.'

' "The salt of the earth." What did he mean by that?'

Quick as a flash, I replied, 'Salt prevents meat from rotting.'

Phinney raised his eyebrows. 'I can see you have been well educated', he said, puffing on his cigarette.

'He smokes,' I thought. 'A true Christian doesn't smoke.' No doubt because no one smokes in the New Testament.

Occasionally, when it was my turn, I was sent to a place called Neuvilly. I say a place since there was nothing left of the village except a pile of stones and the corner of the ground floor of what had been a house. Next to this ruin there was a small barn. At least, that is all I saw of it, for we had been ordered not to go beyond a certain line marked by a post. When I first saw it, I was transfixed by this desolate landscape. I have forgotten why, but I was alone and so I drew the ambulance to a halt. I think that what affected me most was the extraordinary hush, and the expression 'the silence of death' came to my mind. There was nothing. Life was simply absent. The grey sky was empty, the earth was naked, no bird sang.

Inside the ruin which served as a first-aid post, it was rather different. This is my strangest memory of the entire war. Just in front of a cellar, which I shall mention again later, there were three steps which led to a door which I was always happy to open. I found myself in the presence of a Frenchman in blue uniform who shook my hand very warmly. I believe he was an officer although I was never quite sure. It was Lieutenant Jabin. Once he realized I spoke his language as well as he did, he expressed his delight in a rather literary manner. After enquiring very briefly what I had done before the war (which was quickly related), he took down from a shelf a copy of Albert Samain's poems and for the next quarter of an hour, with great enthusiasm, he recited verse, accompanying his reading with expressive gestures. He was, as I remember, a very pale man in his forties with a large body and a rather thin face. When he was not speaking he hummed. It was clear from his behaviour that he was determined to banish all thought of war, at least within the confines of the room in which we found ourselves. I can't remember how the room was furnished apart from an armchair, a few red plush chairs and a fairly long table which, a few minutes later, was to be an object of astonishment for me.

Taking advantage of a brief pause, I asked Lieutenant Jabin where I should park my ambulance.

'It's true, I hadn't thought about that. In the barn. Try not to make too much noise.'

I have forgotten to mention, in fact, that this was one of the instructions we had been given. So I left the room and found my vehicle on the road. Dusk was falling but one could still see clearly, and with so many words still buzzing in my ears, the silence of the landscape and the sky outside seemed full of menace. As quietly as I could, I steered the ambulance into the barn.

Someone was there. In front of me, almost at my feet, a soldier lay on a stretcher. I pulled up immediately. His cloak had been thrown over his head and chest, and his white, youthful hands had been carefully placed on either side of his body. His legs and feet had been stretched out in the same way. I went to park the ambulance at the back of the barn and then came back to look at the soldier. I shall never be able to express the emotions that welled up inside me at that moment. Sadness and fury were mingled simultaneously with love. Those hands were almost the hands of a little boy and those slender fingers could hardly have been able to hold a rifle. And underneath the military cloak, what was there? I didn't want to know; I just looked at this slightly built, still body which was enveloped in an extraordinary silence and a solitude which my presence could not disturb. There was such anguish in my heart and I am not ashamed to say that tears rolled down my cheeks; tears of compassion no doubt, but they were very like the tears of love, and from that moment a hatred of war became fixed in my heart forever. I vowed never to kill, even to defend myself, and I asked God to be witness to my promise.

Back in Lieutenant Jabin's strange little room, I was surprised to see that during my absence the table had been laid for dinner, for I did not think I had been out for long, but what surprised me even more and delighted me, was that the table had been covered with a fine white tablecloth. A tablecloth suggested peacetime and my parents' home.

We sat down to eat almost immediately. I have no memory of the meal, which was cooked by the lieutenant's orderly. I do remember the cook, however, and I seem to see him again now as I write. He was a tall, jolly, red faced man. The Americans in our section never called him anything but Doucement because '*doucement*' [slow down] was what he said whenever he was driven at great speed by them in their ambulances. This man with all his experience of fighting at the front was terrified in our vehicles. Furthermore, he was an incorrigible boozer. Anyway, Doucement served us, and then disappeared into the cellar. My host began to recite poetry and to reminisce about the Avenue Victor Hugo where he lived before the war. I said a few words about the Rue Cortambert, since my home was roughly in the same neighbourhood, but they went unheeded. Paris seemed so lovely yet so far away.

Towards the end of dinner, I felt I should compliment my host on the quality and whiteness of his tablecloth.

'Yes,' he said, 'I've got some equally fine sheets and I'll tell you why: they are shrouds which the government feels obliged to send me in which to bury the poor chaps who give up the ghost in this place. I ask you, what do they need them for? Well, so that they are not wasted. . . I've got a pile of them. Do you want a couple for the night? No? Just as you wish.'

I thought of the boy lying on the stretcher and could only bow my head. It crossed my mind that Lieutenant Jabin was mad, that the war had made him mad, and Samain's poems which had been recited in this ghastly little ruin began to take on a sinister aspect. When I thought I had stayed long enough, I asked the lieutenant to excuse me and I went to bed in the room that had been reserved for me: that is to say, in the cellar. By the light of my torch, I found some blankets thrown over a stretcher: it was my bed. There was no question of undressing. I lay down and tried to pull myself together. I had scarcely closed my eyes when the noise of someone shouting made me jump up: '*Doucement!*'

My friends had warned me. Doucement shared the cellar with me and the sounds of his nightmares, which were not helped by his getting plastered every night, echoed around the room. Did he think he was in an ambulance skidding along a bombed road on two wheels? That is what I imagined, and I went back to sleep with the covers pulled up carefully over my left ear.

The fact that I spent a rather unsettled night was partly due to Doucement whose voice made me wince in my sleep, but also because from time to time I felt something creeping over my shoulder and all over my body, that seemed to come and go, and gradually a curious link seemed to be established between my companion's yells and whatever it was that was moving over me. When dawn came, I opened my eyes and noticed that once again there were huge rats running around the room, though I was too weary even to shudder. They probably slept here during the day; by night, however, they frolicked around this cellar and ran freely over our bodies. I have never seen rats of such a size.

I quickly covered my head and drew my feet up tightly, only moving when I felt one of them on my back. I was not bitten. Meanwhile, Lieutenant Jabin, I imagined, was sleeping rather more comfortably under his shroud in the dining-room.

On one occasion, and I cannot now remember the reason, I was sent on my own to the village of Souilly. I recollect that there were a great number of railway lines and a large hospital, and in front of the hospital there was a vast red cross, laid out in red pebbles against a background of small white stones within an enormous circle, which was no doubt visible from a great height. It was there, under a grey sky, that I experienced certain moments that have marked me most deeply. It seemed to me that all the sadness in the world was gathered in that place. What I had experienced the previous year at the Ritz hospital in Paris, where two of my sisters had worked as nurses, was almost nothing compared to what I felt at that moment when I suddenly recognized the futility of earthly things. Quite simply, happiness was no longer possible. Hatred alone had triumphed, and despair, too. Something froze within me and I don't know how long it was before I could move. I remained transfixed by some sort of inner revelation and a sense of terror seized me. How can I put it otherwise? It was a panic-stricken fear of this world, of the earthly kingdom, of humanity itself. I had the impression that I had become separated from myself, from all hope in the future, from all joy, and the thought that all was lost took over my mind in the same way that an enemy captures surrendered land. Even today, I wonder what sense such an experience can have had. Where did such sadness come from? Certainly not from God, for God does not frighten those he protects, but there can be no doubt that it rather caused me to cut myself off and take refuge within myself where I could shelter from such a powerful threat, the threat of everything around us, of human hostility, of watchful death. I felt for my rosary deep in my pocket, but there was no question of praying: I wasn't capable of it. Strangely enough, we are often unable to pray just at the moment we most need to do so.

Back at Clermont, I found my colleagues in good spirits. One day one of them said to me with a wink, 'A. Piatt is on his way.' I discovered that A. Piatt was an American army officer charged with inspecting the ambulance sections to find out if any wretched deserters had found their way among us. At least, that was what some of us reckoned, but I believe it was simply a question of integrating all the voluntary services within the American Army. In any case, A. Piatt was travelling by car, searching for our ambulance sections all over the front line.

That morning, as it happened, a car drew up in front of the house and someone shouted, 'That's A. Piatt coming for Green!' The American Army actually took no one under the age of eighteen and I was only just seventeen.

A. Piatt looked harsh and thin in his uniform, with small black eyes that bulged, like a crayfish wearing a pince-nez. I reported to him and in a very nasal voice he asked me my date of birth. I told him.

'Pack your kit', he told me. 'You must leave tomorrow, you are going back home.'

I do not recall anything of my departure. I don't even know whether I was happy about it, but I can remember clearly the compartment of the train in which I travelled the next morning. We were all huddled together and my fellow passengers were laughing, singing and chattering in their sky-blue uniforms for they were returning from the front at Verdun. The thought that in a few hours they would be in Paris gave their gaiety a chilling quality rather like the behaviour of someone who is condemned to death and who is then suddenly released. They were fooling around like children and enjoying themselves with all the abandon that leads to drunkenness. Perhaps that is the best way of describing their behaviour: they were drunk with happiness.

I must have caught the train at Clermont, whereas they got on at Dombasle. At first they looked at me in amazement. My youth (I still looked like a boy) and my khaki uniform needed some explanation. I was the first American they had seen, yet I spoke French just like them. When, in reply to their questions, I told them that I had joined up before I was seventeen, they looked at each other and burst out laughing, and one of them, the youngest and the biggest tease, put a finger to his forehead. He was a very good looking boy who had the accent and all the banter of a Parisian. Sitting directly in front of me, he made a fool of himself to amuse his friends who seemed to be very much under his influence. With his elbows and knees stretched out and his fingertips on his thighs, he asked me whether I didn't think he looked dandy in his carefully brushed uniform. I felt very intimidated by him, for in my eyes he had all the glamour of someone who had fought at the front, and I cannot remember what I said to him; probably nothing. At one station where the train stopped, he leant out of the window and asked a woman who was selling newspapers,

'Excuse me madam, do you have *La Croix*?' [a Catholic newspaper]

This question, which brought him further laughter, disturbed me without my knowing quite why, before it occurred to me that perhaps the boy was an unbeliever and, since he was smiling at me in a friendly way and was no longer bothering me, I began to wonder how he could be saved. I might have kept some of this concern, let it be said in passing, for my own salvation, but I never even imagined that there would not be a place for me in Heaven and I was only concerned about the salvation of others.

Back home, I found a sad place. My father's hair was now greying and sorrow had aged him.* He told me that an American officer had come to discuss my position with him and had said that if I wanted to stay in the ambulance service all I had to do was to tell them that I was eighteen and not seventeen. To which my father had replied, rising to his feet,

'My son is not a liar, sir. If you don't want him, send him back to me. Now go!'

I wondered what I should do. It was almost winter and the apartment was already freezing. I sat at the dining-room table and opened my books again; books on philosophy so I could find out what was being taught at the lycée, but I never managed to become the person I had been before I left home. With some astonishment I noticed that I missed my companions: their youth, their carefree ways, even the foul language which I didn't always understand,

* Julian Green's mother had died at the end of 1914. [See *The Green Paradise*] (*Tr.*)

but which was always accompanied by a reassuring gaiety. Nevertheless, I was not bored. The chapel of our neighbours, the White Sisters, seemed the most beautiful place to me and I never tired of hearing the nuns chanting the Psalms. In a hell-bent world they continued to sing to God's glory. With them I felt that I was saved and, if I am not mistaken, I started to go to communion again every morning.

Is that how it was at the time? I suppose so. In any case, I do remember that in a very dark room at the back of the apartment, which we tried to keep warm by lighting a few logs in the chimney, I saw my sister Retta for the last time. She was in bed and seemed to me to be thin, but still just as beautiful, with her long black hair and her cheeks which were still pink.

'Come here', she said to me, 'turn to the light.' She studied me carefully for a long time and made a few jokes which I have forgotten. She was wearing a pale pink, woollen morning-coat and her gestures were already those of someone who is frightened of straining herself, yet she laughed, and in her innocence she gave me a present of a book she had had bought for me. It was not a devotional book because she found me a little too serious; it was a collection of de Maupassant's short stories which she had no doubt not read and which she must have thought were inoffensive stories about hunting: the *Contes de la Bécasse*.

I cannot think of these things without a pang of pain. 'Why is she ill?', I would ask myself. 'Why her? She is so young, so beautiful and so good. . .' A few weeks later she went back to the hospital at Neuilly for further operations, but I had already left.

My father had discovered that an ambulance service, subsidised by the Morgan Harjes bank in New York, was being formed on the Italian front. This independent army organization would accept my services, and so without even stopping to discuss the matter, I went to sign on at their offices in the Rue François 1er. I was given a uniform very like the one I had been wearing, and towards the middle of December that year, I found myself in a small hotel room in Milan.

This account is in some sense an indictment of the young man I once was, but it is written as a reaction against certain autobiographies which seem to me to be largely untrue. Most confesssions contain vital omissions for which the authors seem to have given themselves absolution. I don't say they are wrong to absolve themselves but I wish they felt more ashamed for having left out minor details they preferred not to reveal. For my part, I could say a little more to justify myself, offering in support my total lack of direction during these formative years, but I think this will be obvious to the reader without my boring him with constant reminders.

I realize, however, that I have moved ahead too fast and I must go back a few weeks. One evening in November 1917, I was sitting studying, surrounded by books (I always needed a great many of them), when there was a knock at the front door and I thought of Jeanne Lepêcheur's visit* a year ago, but this was not Jeanne, it was Mr Ware.

He walked into the room stealthily, making a face that could be taken for a smile. Sitting down opposite me, he made a short speech in his rather brusque voice, meticulously choosing his words in a manner reminiscent of an academic, for there was something quite stylish about this proud man. I remember that his cap, thrown down on the

* See *The Green Paradise*

table between us, looked as if it had been battered by the winds of the battlefield, and I think he carried a switch-stick. None of this intimidated me. I was polite and Mr Ware was in my home.

'They want to give you a decoration,' he told me.

I opened my mouth in astonishment. "A decoration? Why?'

'Oh, it's because of this business of the ambulance which you took instead of your own. Not that there was anything unusual about that.'

I agreed with him entirely and told him so.

He gave a tigerish smile. 'In any case, I haven't done anything more about it.'

'You're quite right,' I exclaimed.

How relieved I was to utter these words which redeemed me as far as I was concerned! In fact, I think he had been expecting rather a different reaction and here was I asking him and his decoration to get lost. He raised his eyebrows and went on:

'In any case, I don't need to remind you that we do not usually accept foreign decorations.' (This was no doubt true at the time but they soon changed this rule). 'And after all', he concluded, 'the rest of us don't need a medal pinned onto our uniform just because we have done our duty, do we?'

There again I warmly agreed with him and so, the conversation completed, he got up and took his leave.

Left on my own, I reasoned that it would have been ridiculous to give me a decoration when I was quite sure that I had done nothing to deserve one, but because the United States had only been at war for a short time they were looking for American chests on which they could pin a medal. It is what they call making a gesture and its only purpose was symbolic. Having said all this, however, I must admit that if they had decorated me, even undeservedly, I would have felt incredibly proud. Nevertheless, I took great pleasure in disappointing Monsieur Ouaire who, I am sure, had been expecting me to react rather differently. On the other hand, he was from the North and he knew I was a Southerner (more than a little proud of the fact). Had he wished to humiliate me, he now knew that he could have saved himself the trouble, but for fear of anyone making fun of me, I kept this decoration business a secret.

In Milan then, in December 1917, I found myself alone in one of the saddest little hotel rooms anywhere in the world. It was not so much that it was poorly furnished, as cramped and cluttered, with large, dark pieces of furniture. A wretched little lamp with a pink shade battled in vain with the gathering shadows. In this depressing atmosphere I went to bed and gave way to a pleasureless temptation out of some sort of inexplicable need. I think that the mere fact of being in Italy led me to committing a sin which I no longer thought about any more. I hesitate to write these words, but the sound of Italian voices had a strong corrupting effect on me; it seemed to me that they only spoke of carnal pleasures. Whatever the reason, my action filled me with sadness and, following Baudelaire's advice, I switched out the little light and hid in the darkness.

The next day before dawn, I wandered about the dim streets of this enormous city with my pack on my back. Never having had the slightest sense of direction, I got lost, but I had at least an hour to spare before my appointment and a feeling of pure joie de vivre had me singing to myself in a low voice while I meandered aimlessly around. At the corner of a street I stopped an old man dressed in peasant clothes and asked him the way to the Via Solferino. 'The

Via Choulferino', he repeated. With gestures that I understood better than his language, he showed me the way and I was easily the first to arrive at the assembly point.

I soon found myself inside a vast electric-lit garage full of ambulances, surrounded by about twenty boys whom I had never met before and whose sleepy faces looked as if they were still half-dreaming. Questions such as 'Where do you come from?', or more often, 'What state are you from?' were on everyone's lips. Many of the boys were boasting about the marvellous night they had spent after dining at Covas's. I didn't know what Covas was, but in my imagination I saw it as a brightly lit place where scenes such as those you can see in the complicated drawings of Giulio Romano and Albano took place. Almost all the boys had been sinful, but then so had I. Each time I had to explain to one or another of them that I was an American even though I was born in Paris, I felt a little more lonely.

At last a plump, tubby-shaped man appeared, warmly clad against the cold in a coat with a fur collar. Our boss, Mr Ware, I thought, would have looked at him with such disdain. That, a leader? More like a woman. He told us that these ambulances were not for us. They were Fiats, a name that has stuck in my mind because of the words *fiat voluntas tuas*' in the Lord's Prayer. Ours were waiting for us at Varese. There were lorries to take us there.

I have completely forgotten what happened next. I only remember that I got lost that night on a road in Lombardy, driving a small grey ambulance which was identical to the one I had driven in the Argonne. It was pouring with rain and in the beam of my headlamps I could distinguish the pretty stone markers that bordered the edge of each side of the road, but where was I? Where was I going? I cannot recall anything that happened apart from stopping at the door of a tall house which was painted pink and which seemed to be a farm.

The door opened, and I was taken into a large room where two or three men and a woman were standing around a fire, and I say 'around' deliberately since the fire had been built on top of what looked like a millstone which lay flat in the middle of the room. The smoke rose to the ceiling, wafting up towards a type of brick chimney built into the roof. Had I known my Roman antiquities better, I would have immediately recognized it as the chimney of an atrium. In any case, in my bumbling Italian I explained that I was American and that I was lost. They then asked me if I had eaten and I replied that I had not. I was dying of hunger.

I dined at the end of a long table, and it was one of the best meals I have ever eaten because it was composed of simple dishes that I loved at that age. I still remember the *osso buco* and the *polenta*, but, above all, the gaiety and kindness of these people who had never met me before yet treated me as if I was a brother or a son. They had sat down a little distance from me so that I should not feel awkward, and behind them in that large rather dark room I saw the fire whose magical presence became an image of their charity.

Everything else I've forgotten. They showed me which road to take and eventually I found my section, but where and at what time I don't know. Two days later, we drove through Padua and arrived the following day at Dolo in the Veneto. The road was lined with villas, some of which were magnificent, and one of them, the Villa Mira, was assigned to us as our quarters for forty-eight hours. It was a long building that was partly a country house and partly a town house, and we were amazed to find ourselves in marble-tiled rooms.

I was rather more astonished by everything than my friends were, because I was in love with Italy. I touched the walls, I would have kissed the ground, but I hid what was a sort of drunkenness through a fear of ridicule. I was overcome with a violent desire to live, a hunger for happiness which made me want to both laugh and cry. I remember that in a nineteenth-century room on the ground floor of this villa, there was a piano at which two of my colleagues played a four-handed piece by Mendelssohn that delighted me, for it expressed all my faith in the future. The war no longer existed, everything around me seemed to be smiling. There was great feeling of sensual elation about it all, not that I would have had it otherwise.

Venice was not far away but, alas, that was not where we were going. Our destination was Roncade, between Mestre and Treviso. I was about to spend five crucial months of my life there.

When a novelist writes his memoirs (if that word applies here) there is often the temptation to create a greater coherence to his memories than truthfulness should allow. I mean to say that, faced with all the gaps that he discovers in his life, he may attempt to fill them in. In my case I am bound to admit that I have only retained isolated fragments of my early life and that I am unable to join all the pieces together. I did not keep my diary then. There are many things that have vanished except, I trust, those that really matter. And yet who is to say if it is not precisely that which is hidden which is in fact the most essential? I sometimes even wonder, thinking along these lines, whether it is not a mistake to keep a daily record of all that we do, and whether it would not be more sensible to allow memory to get on with its job of retaining this and removing that . . . all that.

However much I torture my memory, I can remember next to nothing about Roncade, not even the church, which is surprising. It is true, we had been given the strictest orders about what was out of bounds and the extent to which we should talk to people. We were probably not allowed to go into the town. That is the only possible explanation I can find for the fact that throughout the end of that winter and the spring that followed I did not once go to church. Our orders were not to disturb the local population in any way. I suppose they wanted to avoid any arguments and 'senti-mental' complications. In any case we kept ourselves to ourselves and we were lodged in houses along the road.

I can see very clearly the little villa where I and a few other Americans lived until the spring of 1918. It was very basic: square, with a small terrace and just one floor, solid, comfortable and too simple to be either pretty or ugly. Our boss moved in too, such as it was. Only once, through a half-opened door, did I get the opportunity to have a look at his room on the ground floor. It was very cosy, as one might have expected. There was a fire burning in the hearth and a pale fur rug covered the bed. There were comfortable armchairs to relax in and a pile of magazines to help while away the time. The intoxicating aroma of an expensive cigarette wafted up to me before the door was closed.

For reasons which I can only guess at today, my room was immediately above the boss's, but, needless to say, it had none of that voluptuous *je ne sais quoi* which one could smell in his. Mine was light and spacious, and I dare say it was attractive. The walls were painted a very pale blue. An iron bedstead, a wardrobe with a looking glass, and an upright chair were the only furniture. Because it was Italy, I judged it to be a splendid room. What's more, it was mine. I didn't have to share it with anyone. This is where I first began to suspect something that I failed to grasp for months. The other boys slept two or three to much smaller rooms, but it never occurred to me to ask about this. I did not question my orders for a second. It's also worth pointing out that my room extended out onto the little terrace which I've already mentioned.

The question is, why should they have given me this room, and why did I have it to myself? There can only be two answers to this:

1. No one wanted to be with me. That is possible. To them I was a foreigner who didn't come from any particular state and who spoke with a Southern accent. They all came from the North or the West. They needed time to get used to me.

2. The boss had been asked to keep an eye on me because I was the youngest and, according to him, the most easily led astray (he didn't know me very well). Because of this, I was kept apart from the others so that he could hear anyone coming into or leaving my room.

I don't remember whether the room was heated or not. It was a fairly mild winter and I don't think I felt cold at all.

In another room, which looked out over a landscape of fields and trees rather than the road, were two boys one of whom was in love with the other, although the love was apparently unrequited. The suitor, a gentle, bespectacled beanpole of a boy, whom I shall call James, confided in me and I sympathised with him for I still remembered how I had felt about Frédéric, but the word love was never mentioned. James had refined tastes and read Jane Austen.

We were far from guessing the strange fate that would befall him. In any case, the object of his passion was a well brought up boy, with a smiling pink face and a pointed nose, who was slightly disdainful of me because I had not been born in America, although this was something I only realized much later. Furthermore, what could I have understood about matters which did not concern me? I said to James: 'He's rather a bore, your friend Dick. And he's not going to get through Yale, because he's hardly read a thing.' 'I know all that, alas', sighed James, 'but I can't control my feelings.' Many other similar discussions on this topic took place, but I never guessed what it was that James was actually trying to say. He shared the same room as Dick. What more could he want? 'You don't understand', he said to me. No, really, I didn't. 'Come on. Haven't you lived in Paris?' 'Yes. What's that got to do with it?' He shook his head in despair. Eventually I began to find it all rather tiresome. When one thinks about it, I wonder if anything in the world can be more tedious than a lover, except perhaps in a novel or in a play, and even then. . .

In the room facing mine, on the other side of a marbled corridor, there were some other boys I shall mention again later in order to illustrate the peculiarity of my character which I disguised beneath a gentle demeanour. I was proud, awkward, and deep down, contemptuous of others whom I tended to ridicule ruthlessly. Today, I cannot understand why someone did not give me a good thrashing at the time, but rather in the way that one does not hit a child, my astonishing innocence, which people became aware of quite quickly, must have protected me in some way from violence. They thought I was a little crazy, but in general they put that down to the fact that I was born in Europe. Otherwise, they put up with my teasing in a good-natured way, and my gaiety made them laugh. I was not as withdrawn as I was in France. Something in the Italian air must have gone to my head and I was unaware that all sorts of things were beginning to bubble up inside me.

We had our meals in another house a hundred yards away from the one I have just mentioned. It was a large, beautiful, low building surrounded by trees, orchards and small gardens and I loved its rustic appearance. The huge kitchen was like something out of the Middle Ages, and it smelt of burning logs and of bread being baked. One often saw Italian soldiers there who had come to gossip with the cook, an imposing woman who watched me carefully whenever I happened to be around. One day, I had come to ask her something and we were in the middle of a conversation when the men who were chatting nearby suddenly stopped talking. They were sitting on benches outside but I could hardly see them in the half-light of dusk. Suddenly, in an awkward silence, the cook paid me a compliment in the sort of voice that one reserves for the deaf and for foreigners. I blushed to the roots, not from modesty, but because I thought she was making fun of me in front of the soldiers. Even now, so many years later, I sometimes sigh when I think of this scene. No one moved, no one said a word. I remained glued to the spot like a ninny, then, mumbling some incomprehensible phrase, I ran off. Outside, I hid my face in my hands. This woman had looked so serious when she spoke to me, and none of the soldiers had laughed. . . I walked for a while in the fields which were irrigated with troughs of water which reflected the sunset, and my heart was beating so much I had to lie down. The fear of having made myself appear ridiculous upset me terribly. A less foolish boy would have thanked the woman with a smile and found something amusing to say, but I had run away. I was terrified.

In the dining-room where we all gathered for meals three times a day, apart from our boss who took his in his room, I sat down next to the oldest person in our section. His name was Clarke and his hair was completely white. He was a good and gentle man who shook his head sadly whenever the boys made too much noise. In fact, everyone was always yelling and we ate amid a constant racket. The leader of the bunch was a tall, handsome boy who looked like a football player and who died six months later in France when he was burnt alive in a tank. His name was Dresser and his booming voice rose above the din. Sitting on old Clarke's right, I kept quiet, and I could see that our behaviour upset the Italian soldiers who waited on us in silent indignation, for the boys would often throw bits of bread at each other which in some part of the country was extremely scarce. I felt ashamed in front of these little soldiers in their grey-green uniforms, ashamed at the impression we must have given. Eventually, our boss, in a sudden fit of energy, rose from his fur-covered bed and read out a written order that this rumpus should stop.

The dining-room was bare and tiled with marble, with two windows and a very long white wooden table at which we sat with our backs to the wall. I can remember the noise, the big bowls of macaroni, and also the whiteness of the bread. This bread was actually as white as a communion host and I always fingered it with respect. If there was one thing which upset me in a way I had not quite realized, it was seeing this white bread being rolled up into balls and chucked around the room.

Old Clarke kept an eye on me and spoke to me softly. I

had been placed next to him on purpose and I am ashamed to relate what follows. One evening, I can't remember what the occasion was (perhaps it was New Year's Eve), we were given champagne to drink and many of the boys pretended to be tipsy so that they could shout all the louder. I had only drunk a very little from the half-full glass and it had had no effect on me, no more than it had on my neighbour on my left who wished me a happy New Year and revealed his wonderfully white, even row of teeth when he smiled. What on earth came over me at that moment? So as to seem as crazy as the others and so as to be like them, I waited until he lowered his head and then poured the few drops of champagne that remained in my glass down his neck. I saw the drops roll down his open collar. He gave a start and turned towards me. 'Why did you do that?' he asked in a low voice. He gave me such a sad look that I was quite overcome. I gulped and said, 'I don't know, Mr Clarke. Please forgive me.' He wiped his neck and replied good-humouredly that it didn't matter, but I was still appalled at my foolishness. I had probably wanted to prove to myself that I could also be a devil, but no one had seen what had happened, no one took any notice of me. To all these fortunate young men I was always the 'kid'. In any case, that was the impression I had, and I never stopped feeling humiliated. I was perfectly prepared to do wrong, but something prevented me from ever speaking about it.

Several times a week, just as we did in France, we were sent, either on our own or with a companion, to the first-aid posts or hospitals which might need our services, although at this period there was no fighting on the Italian front. The big Austro-German thrust had been contained and, ever since the autumn, all was calm. During the five months I spent in the Veneto, the only person I had to transport was an Italian soldier suffering from nervous exhaustion.

One evening in January 1918, just as I entering the dining-room, my mail was brought to me: two letters from Paris. I recognized my father's handwriting and withdrew to another room. I still have these letters; wise, sad, resigned, with their very straight lines and carefully chosen words. My sister Retta had died in hospital at Neuilly. She had suffered a great deal but she never complained. Her last words had been a child's prayer, the confident prayer of a child who is about to fall asleep. As she died in the service of France, she was given a military funeral. French soldiers in the Protestant church on the Avenue de l'Alma . . .

I went outside and walked round the house. In the dining-room the boys were laughing and shouting, and for a few moments life no longer had any meaning for me. Retta was only twenty-two. Why did she have to die? Why her, a girl who had only ever done good? Why had she been brought into the world if she was going to have to leave it so soon? I turned these questions over and over in my mind and I felt sorrowful and confused. What justice was there? Or goodness? I didn't dare blame divine providence but I did feel something shatter inside me. I felt very disturbed. I returned to my room and wrote to my father. Only slowly did I register the extent of my grief. In vain I told myself that the news I had been given was incorrect, that Papa had made a mistake. Yet it was true, and it was deeply shocking to me, the more shocking because it was unjust. I did not yet know that every death is shocking and, however much I grieved, I did not shed a single tear.

That winter night that brought the news of my sister's death had all the appearance of spring. There was a sweetness in the air that caressed my face and hands, and in the depths of my sorrow, my body glowed. Holding this letter in my hands, I nevertheless felt happy to be alive. I would be hypocritical or blind if I did not admit this, but I want to go further: it was as if my sadness had been swept away by something in the night air. It is hard to explain the sensation and I reproached myself for being heartless, not realizing that true suffering would come later when I had explored the full extent of what had happened. At the time, and it's easy to understand why, it seemed that the distance separating me from Neuilly alleviated my pain. It was only when I returned to Paris and could no longer see my sister that I understood and really believed she was dead, and it was then that I suffered most. For in the end, what did this letter, this short letter on blue paper, signify? It couldn't be death. Death was absence and I had to touch and see absence if I was to believe. A mere letter could not make my sister any more absent this night than last night. She had not been there the previous evening, and she was no more nor less present now. Nothing had changed here. The boys were laughing as usual. Where was death? Death was unimaginable. I grieved silently. For several days I did not open my mouth.

No one knew what had happened to me. Who would I have told? I could not confide in any of the boys, not even lovesick James. What difference could it make to anyone that my sister was dead? I nevertheless wrote to Father Crété to tell him that Retta was now in Heaven, but his prompt reply chilled me: one could only hope that she was saved. The letter slid from my hand.

Once a week I was sent with my ambulance to a place called Monastier di Treviso. As the name suggests, it was an ancient cloister where the monks, from the time they first came to live here, so it was rumoured, had never exactly behaved themselves. I remember the sombre buildings which reminded one of a castle in a forest. There was a spacious cloister, which was impressive but rather severe, and there was a large room whose ceiling was so high and so dark that one could only see it when one was standing by the window. It was there, by this window, that some extremely polite Italian officers invited me to join them for coffee. One of them, a tall, thin man with a blue chin, clapped his long hands and called out, 'Fiordelmondo!'. This splendid name echoed back and forth across the high walls, and after a certain time a soldier appeared carrying a tray with a coffee pot and six or eight cups. What can we have spoken about? Certainly not the war, which they detested. One day, the tall, thin officer spoke to me in French and told me what it was the monks got up to. At first, as was usual with me, I did not understand what he was talking about; then I told myself that they must be like the monks in Italian fairy tales and I rather began to take against this officer, for deep down inside me I still had the notion, that one day I might also be a monk, and I wanted to be a good one.

One afternoon when I was talking to a soldier in the cloister, a fat, badly dressed officer came up to me. His flabby face was yellowy-green and he had a slightly grumpy expression, but there was something so attentive about his dark eyes that when I looked at him I was unable to speak and I stepped back a little. He walked slowly towards me, his hands in his pockets. There was something about him that made me realize he was the chaplain. Suddenly, he said: '*Lei e buono*'.

Is it not irritating to have to write that I pretended not to understand? In fact, I wanted him to say more. I needed compliments, and such was my vanity that I could not have enough of them. He shrugged his soldiers impatiently and again said, '*Buono*', while at the same time pointing to his heart and to his forehead. I looked at him with an air of polite astonishment and said nothing. I was so self-effacing. . . A moment later, however, how I regretted my deception! This man had misjudged me: he did not know that I was impure, that I made fun of my friends, that I had not even cried when my own sister died. *Buono*, really? This old priest's face has often come back to my mind since then, like that of a messenger.

I seem to remember that on leaving Monastier di Treviso, I passed by a long row of poplars, the like of which I have never seen anywhere else, either for the size of their trunks or for their colossal height. The winter must have been a very mild one, for the yellow autumn leaves were still on the branches, making these enormous trees (I think there were thirty of them) look like huge leather candlesticks.

My sense of *joie de vivre* was so strong that it banished any feelings of sadness and whenever I was alone I had a strong urge to sing as I did when I was a child. On the roads, in my ambulance, I sang so much that I made myself hoarse. Once, after it had been raining for a long time, I was sent off to some first-aid post and discovered to my delight that the surrounding countryside had been so badly flooded that the roads were covered in sheets of water. The land around had become a vast mirror that reflected the sky. I felt as if I were locked in a dream from which I would not awake. I am not sure why driving over water when one is on land should be quite so magical, but it was a wonderful experience and several times in the years that followed I would dream that I was running over the surface of clear, crystal water. I would want to cry out with joy as if, freed from the weight of my body, I had been transformed into a spirit with only the outward appearance of a body. Naturally, I greeted the flooding with every song that came into my head.

Two or three times a week I would be given leave, or orders, to report at Mestre but I can recall nothing about this town (it has been bombed out of my memory) apart from the station, which I shall mention again later, and a large square at the end of which was a newspaper kiosk. If I remember this kiosk, it is because this was where I used to buy French novels by the armful, four or five at a time, in an illustrated edition at 95 centimes each. I would read one a day, no more, no less. Today, I wonder what it was that I found so thrilling about them. Principally, I suppose, they provided reasons for no longer believing in sin. For me that was the main lesson I learnt from the naturalists and all the novelists that succeeded them. After reading all those stories of adultery, intimate relationships and passing fancies which, in any case, I did not understand, I concluded that physical love was the great affair in life and that the catechism, according to many of these intelligent and highly gifted men, was really only for women, and children and half-wits. 'If you weren't wearing skirts, you'd get a couple of smacks on your clerical face!' That was how one of de Maupassant's characters speaks to a priest who had caused him to miss a rendezvous with a pretty woman. The phrase made me shudder and I never forgot it. For others, devout people were figures of fun. One felt sorry for them and smiled rather condescendingly when referring to them. So that was how religion was seen in the eyes of the world, a world where only sensuality and success mattered — not that I had much more than a confused notion about either. For instance, just at the point where one was anticipating some useful information about the pleasures of the flesh, the author would suppress it, as if taking it for granted that everyone knew it all — yet I did not know. Those erotic drawings I had seen in 1916 did not seem to belong to the same universe as the works of de Maupassant, the

Goncourt brothers or Zola. When one of them, I'm not sure which, wrote: 'He possessed her on the floor', I wondered what 'possessed' could possibly mean. When Claude Farrère used the term physical pleasure, I was none the wiser. These clever obscenities retained their mystery for me. I was disappointed and rather sad. Because I had not done any of these things, I felt that I was not yet a man.

From the room in which I read these books, I could see a road along which women would sometimes pass by dressed in enormous black shawls that reached to their ankles. 'Are they what one would call beautiful women?' I would ask myself. They walked past like statues in a dream and never stopped. Did they get up to such wickedness? I wondered how any sensual pleasures might come about for they looked so dignified and severe that one could not possibly imagine them behaving recklessly. Would one have to topple over these statues in order to possess them on the floor? Perhaps other novels would clarify how it all happened, but I had quite a time selecting first this novel, then that one, Signora, and then this one again, for they were all equally obscure.

There was no table in my room. I bought myself one in Mestre. It was just big enough for a book and my elbows. When I was not reading, I used to sit carving notches into this piece of furniture with a knife. The wood was soft and cut easily. I ruined the little table. A friend pointed this out to me and I answered curtly that it was mine. I could actually say that I owned it. Why did I behave in this way? These notches appalled me. It looked as if an animal had gnawed down one side of the table, yet there was something within me that drove me to mutilate it. In a frenzy, with my tongue between my teeth, I would shave off slivers of wood, which flew around the room.

As for the novels with their dull illustrations, I believe I stacked them inside the wardrobe with the mirror. It is time I mentioned this wardrobe.

I think it must have been in February. Around that time there had been several days of soft, spring-like weather. Returning to my room one evening after dinner, I had a sudden urge to look at myself naked in the mirror. It was something I had never done before. It is hard to believe that at the age of seventeen I should have had such a vague idea of what I looked like *in naturalibus*. I knew the individual parts, but not the overall picture. It is because of this that I can judge the full effect of those early lessons which led me to place the sight of nakedness on the same plane as impurity. You can only see yourself properly if you stand back a little, otherwise you have the same impression of yourself as an artist might have of a model sitting on his knees! I suppose I lacked curiosity, and it is true that I was only curious as far as my face was concerned. The human body did not interest me. I had not looked at my brother-in-law when he made me jump into the sea with him the previous summer in Italy, because one should not look at a naked person. I should also add that I had absolutely no desire to do so. From the paintings of Albano and Giulio Romano I mainly retained the facial expressions, which if I remember correctly expressed very little apart from a mild boredom. Be that as it may, it was a very sudden impulse, and as I took off my clothes I knew that I was doing something wrong.

My heart was pumping furiously and in one of those flashes of self-deception that we indulge in, I wondered why that should be, as if I had no idea of what I was about to do. Did I not undress every evening? This evening, however, I was frightened of every movement I made.

Once I was completely naked, I bravely turned my eyes towards the mirror and my fears vanished. The sense of terror that had hovered over me was replaced by an extraordinary calm. For the first time in my life I observed the nakedness of a human being, and that person was myself. A strange delight flowed through me as I observed that I was slim and well-built, but the sensation only lasted for a second, for a sudden irresistible force threw me forward and most of my body was now pressed against the mirror. The cold, flat surface had the same effect on me as if a jug of water had been thrown in my face and I drew back immediately, alarmed at what I had just done, not just because of the sin which I believed I had committed, but because it occurred to me that I had behaved like a madman and that perhaps I was indeed mad, like my Uncle Willie who died of venereal disease in 1895. I slipped between the sheets and switched off the light so that the darkness could blot out this disturbing scene. What bothered me most, and what I could not get out of my mind, was that I had pressed my own lips to their reflected image, and try as I might to persuade myself this was not the case, I knew what I had done.

With the hindsight of many years, my behaviour that evening no longer seems so odd. Which human being has not done what I did, or something similar, at one or other moment of his or her life? I remember that the sight of myself in the nude stopped me in my tracks for a moment or two. At the age of seventeen, one's body is more or less fully developed and I had never seen anyone of the same age stripped of his clothes. I was reminded of the statues in the Louvre that my mother had taken me to see and whose beauty had had such an effect on me. They were only made of stone, however, while this much more mysterious substance, flesh, was fully displayed for my admiration; my own flesh, which I told myself no one must ever touch. Did any good come out of all that? I am not sure, but I think so. I vaguely perceived that the flesh was not something to be despised, but that instead it possessed some sort of divine protection that forbade desire.

Not that I really knew what desire was. I had forgotten about it since childhood. I had experienced it painfully at the time (as I have described in an earlier book*), but in February 1918 I was barely capable of noticing what distinguished one person from another and there was no one who was capable of hurting my feelings. Except for a heady moment in January 1915 and that flash of joy which I have never experienced since, I knew nothing about voluptuousness, that mistress of the world, apart from what novelists had to say — and they are an imaginative breed.

It was about that time that small groups of three or four of us were given permission to spend a day in Venice. I had managed to travel on my own, and from the moment I set foot in the Piazza San Marco, I thought I was going out of my mind. Nothing I had seen on this earth had ever struck me as being as beautiful as this city, which man will one day destroy precisely because it is too beautiful. The air was mild and I saw everything through a haze of powerful sunlight. I roamed from street to street as if I were possessed, carrying a map which I never used for I preferred to lose myself, and all I can recollect from these wanderings is a memory of exhilaration. Twelve years later, I saw Venice again but it was no longer the same city because I was no longer the same person. Aged twenty-

* See *The Green Paradise*

eight or twenty-nine, I could stay as long as I pleased, I could consult guide-books and take rides on gondolas to my heart's content. Alas! I was no longer mad then, nor poor, nor obliged to report back before nightfall or risk punishment. During that day in 1918, I was intoxicated by everything my eyes saw, except for people's faces, to which I paid no attention whatsoever. In the golden gloom of San Marco I momentarily rediscovered the fervour of earlier days, though once I was outside again I soon felt myself lured back into the world's magic. That world was not the dark and sinister place I read about in *The Imitation of Christ*; in Venice the world celebrated the glory of the world and my heart beat only with happiness.

Back in my room that evening I did not even bother to look at the wardrobe mirror. Throwing myself on my bed, I buried my head in my arms, and with my eyes tightly shut, I tried to recreate that lost splendour. It had vanished forever. That first moment would never return. I didn't know that; I didn't know anything.

Dazzled as I had been by Venice and thoroughly intoxicated with art and poetry, I must nevertheless have looked into a shop or two and, as Father Crété would have said, I could not resist the impulse to slip into a bookshop to purchase an English translation of the *Decameron*. I was still obsessed with Boccacio. Now, the extraordinary thing about this little detail is that I would never have believed it and would certainly have forgotten all about it, had I not the actual copy of the book in front of me as I write. It was published by Chatto & Windus and bound in red leather (so I cannot have been exactly poor at the time, but all my pay went on books, and once the money was spent I had nothing left). On the flyleaf, I can see inscribed in the large handwriting I had at the time; a little untidy, rather vain — those capital letters — and a bit aggressive: Julian Green, Venice, 1918.

I no longer remember what impression I had from reading the book again except that I found the final tale of patient Griselda rather tedious, although I recall quite clearly that one day George Dresser, seeing that the book under my arm was Boccacio, let out a loud yell, grabbed my copy and told his friends that he was going to read them one of the more lurid passages from this masterpiece which he knew well.

Here we have a fine example of that well-known Anglo-Saxon hypocrisy. Dresser flicked through the pages impatiently. At last he reached the passages which he was going to read for everyone's delectation. Oh! the anger and disappointment. The discreet translator had left them in Italian. I had read the passages as if I had been reading French, for although I did not speak Italian well I could read it quite fluently (although I certainly didn't tell them that), and Dresser handed the book back to me saying that the translation was useless.

To crown his frustration there was a brief footnote explaining that Boccacio was describing a magic ceremony that was too involved to interest English-speaking readers and that it was preferable to leave these passages in the original. 'A magic ceremony!' roared Dresser. 'You'd have to send the Devil to Hell for this, and do you know what that means?' Poor Dresser. How he laughed, in spite of his disappointment. I would not have remembered any of these things if this particular copy of the book had not brought it all back to me, and now I see him again, this big, proud, ruddy-faced boy with his shining blue eyes and his golden locks curling over his small, determined forehead. Three or four more months of good humour, laughter, singing and banging his fists on the table, drinking bouts and love affairs, and he would perish in flames on the Somme.

At the beginning of March we were all given ten days leave. We could spend it wherever we pleased. The Italian government provided free travel. I chose to go and visit my sister Eleanore in Genoa and I arrived there with my mind tainted once more by Boccacio.

The weather was cold in Genoa and, seen from my sister's apartment, the view of the vast, tragic landscape seemed even more beautiful than it had on my last visit, and it perfectly suited my own grandiose and romantic mood of the time. I compared the dark, windswept clouds with my own inner torment. So what was it that tormented me? Nothing really. At times, I was bothered by my curiosity to know more about this certain pleasure of which I remained ignorant and which I heard people speak about, or read about in second-rate books, but generally I did not feel particularly troubled. Occasionally, I was impatient to *know*, but I didn't suffer. Everything was still dormant within me. Nevertheless, I needed an inner torment of my own in order to prove to myself that I was growing up. I would imagine such noble sorrows. The memory of Chopin's *Nocturnes* which Mademoiselle Jeanne used to play for me was the perfect vehicle to inspire a melancholy I was proud to display. Oh! the foolishness of that age! Father Crété wrote to me at the time: 'For God's sake, my friend, do snap out of the doldrums.' He did not realize that what I wanted was to be a famous and unhappy poet. None of this, however, prevented me from experiencing sudden, and much more honest, moments of gaiety. I wrote a great deal, I started novels that I could not finish, which were filled with tenderness, sensuality and grieving souls. I was devoted to despair. Characters would throw themselves under trains as in *Anna Karenina*. They would drink poison as in *Madame Bovary*. They would seize each other passionately as in de Maupassant, but there I was a little less sure of myself, and I have to admit, restrained by some deep-rooted horror of describing things that were improper. He's a complex creature, a virgin boy!

I wonder if I am not recounting all this in order to delay the hardest moment of these confessions. Yet, I must come to it in the end. For reasons which I have forgotten, my sister had to go away for a day or two and I was alone in the big house with my brother-in-law whom I only saw at meal times. Even then he did not always return for dinner, which meant that I would eat on my own. Pretty Teresina would serve me at table and the *signorino*, as she called me, would comport himself with exemplary gravity. I sometimes regretted that I could not go back to Nervi to have another look at Mr Kreyer's library, but the owner of the villa only stayed there in the summer.

Now, when I say that I was alone in the house that is not strictly true. Apart from Teresina and the cook, who went to bed early, there was someone else, a young lady by the name of Lola.

I realize that this account is taking on the false air of a Casanova but I cannot help it. A rather odd Casanova, as we shall see. The girl in question was my brother-in-law's secretary and one evening — why? I really don't know — it was decided that she would spend the night at our house instead of going home to her parents as she certainly would normally have done, but perhaps they were away. There must have been some reason. In any case, she had supper with me (no exact recollection) and a bed was made up for her in a room adjoining the dining-room. My brother-in-law was not returning until later. Lola was a sensible young girl and everyone knew that the *signorino* was also very sensible, perhaps too much so.

I am not sure why one tends to confide in sensible people. Sometimes they are much more dangerous than others. Often, they are crazy. Lola was pretty, though rather pale, with a round face and nice eyes. She must have been my age or a year older. I was suddenly struck with the idea of doing with her what Boccacio's characters did, and the notion thrilled me. It was after dinner, I believe. The moment could not have been more propitious. The servants were no longer about. Lola had retired to the room which I have just mentioned. I only had to wait until she got into bed, then enter the room and set about my task.

I listened at her door, then when the moment came, without any hesitation I knocked. She must have thought that it was Teresina and told me to come in, but when she saw it was me a sudden fear came over her, for she was lying down and pulled the covers over her breasts. I sat down immediately at the edge of her bed in such a way that I only had to lean down to kiss her. Should I add that I was in uniform? My uniform always produced a certain effect and this time I was depending on it. Moreover, I was so vain that it never occurred to me for a moment that this girl might reject me.

She reproached me for coming into her room in this way, but her reproval was fairly gentle. I paid her a few compliments and asked her whether it upset her to see me sitting beside her. No? Why? She answered by stroking my cheek with her hand: '*Perche ti voglio bene.*'(Because I like you very much). The tenderness with which she spoke these and other words should have made me pause to think a little, but I was rough, selfish and proud. I took hold of the covers which her hands held up to cover herself — though they did not cover quite enough of her — and told her that I wanted to see her entirely naked. She struggled a little. I was sure that eventually she would succumb and that in the end it would be as it was in the books, as it was in Boccacio, but something happened which I had not foreseen. Suddenly, we heard a noise which froze us with horror: the door to the hall had just been opened. My brother-in-law had returned. I only had time to say to Lola: 'I'll come back soon when he's gone to bed'. She put a finger to her lips and I disappeared.

I disappeared with amazing speed. Even today, I wonder how I could have reached my room, taken off my clothes and jumped into bed so quickly that when my brother-in-law half-opened the door a few seconds later, he found me snuggled up under the covers and apparently fast asleep.

Having closed the door, he went back to his bedroom which was next to mine and I listened to him moving around for a few moments. When I heard him removing his shoes, I knew that I would not have long to wait before going back to Lola, but all of a sudden, as if from the effects of a drug, I fell into a deep sleep from which I only awoke at about eight o'clock the next day.

I cannot remember what my feelings were when I woke up that morning, but I have the impression that I felt entirely indifferent. It would be pleasant to be able to write that I fell prey to a nameless passion, for I would be acknowledging a normal, human impulse, but I was not always human. Obsessed with my own being, I was unable to leave the prison which, without realizing it, I had created for myself.

What I cannot conceal is that the deep sleep into which I fell probably changed the whole course of my life. It seems evident to me now that if I had had my way with Lola, I would probably have been a different person, but this is not yet the moment to speak of matters which would only be decided six years later. Was Lola a virgin? I have reason to think not. She would have revealed to me a world I did not know, instead of which I was thrown back inside myself for a whole period of my youth.

And Lola, what did she think of me? She is dead. I will never know. The next day, or the day after, I met her in a street which ran down beneath the Via Assarotti. She probably thought me rather brazen and she must have supposed that I had a good deal of experience. How astonished she would have been if she had known the truth! I went straight up to her and paid her a compliment: '*Come sei bella oggi!*' ('How beautiful you look today.' It was as far as my Italian went.) She reproached me gently for my behaviour on the previous night, or the one before, and I remember she told me that I only thought about *cose indecente*. I replied frankly that she was not mistaken. She laughed and called me a *cattivo* (naughty boy), but I could see that she did not dislike me, for she asked whether we could meet again. 'Certainly', I said like the lout that I was, 'and we shall do some of those things which you mentioned a moment ago.' I cannot remember anything else from this conversation. I cannot even recall whether she asked me why I had not come back to keep her company (that was the expression she had used when I was sitting on her bed), but I can still see the dingy street and the girl with the milky-white skin, and if it is true that our whole life passes before us in detail before we leave this earth, I expect I will see them again on my deathbed.

In fact, I was never to meet Lola again. I suppose my leave came to an end. A few months later, my sister Eleonore mentioned in passing that the girl no longer came to the house and was looking for another job. 'Why did she leave?' I asked. Her reply was curious. 'She said we were not fond enough of her.' 'She must have been in love with me', I thought with my usual modesty.

Here, I must add a few words in parenthesis. The old dreamer who is writing these memoirs insinuates more than once that he was good-looking and caused a few flutters in several hearts. I say 'insinuates' deliberately, as a way of showing how absurd it would be to present myself as a Don Juan. Some explanation is necessary. I knew many boys of my own age, like Roger, my schoolfriend in Paris, for example, who struck me as being far better looking than myself. In my case, I reckoned that viewed from the front, I was handsome, but ugly in profile. Furthermore, my hair was black. Now, the notion was firmly fixed in my mind that one could not really be handsome unless one was blond. Roger was the one splendid exception to this — although I was well satisfied with my own eyes, which I considered wonderful, and by my well-formed mouth, even though it was rather full and I should have preferred fine, ascetic lips. It is impossible to explain these crazy contradictions: I wanted to be both a Greek god and a Catholic saint at one and the same time. In truth, beneath my serious, reasonable exterior I was actually slightly mad. As it happened, I had, thank heavens, a pleasant complexion and a strong, healthy body, although my legs were not quite straight, which made me rather shy. And I was paid a few compliments, which I stored away in my mind. So much for these ridiculous details about which no more need be said. I think it is less hypocritical to mention these things than to allow people to believe something which is not quite accurate. I was hardly an Apollo, but I was reasonably attractive, that's all.

I was attractive because I was young and looked even younger, but it is only through memory that I have become aware of the attraction I exercised on certain people, as I shall explain later. As far as my eyes were concerned, if they were fine I can say the same for many other people's.

Which seventeen-year-old's face, however banal, is not redeemed by the marvel of the human eye? I wonder whether there is anything in the entire universe — any flower, any ocean — that can compare with it. In the brilliance of it inimitable colours it is, perhaps, the masterpiece of creation. The sea is not deeper. In the depths of this tiny jewel we glimpse the most mysterious thing in the world, the human soul, and no one soul is exactly like another. In this sense, each soul is unique. The eye's pupil can exert such a fascination precisely because within it so much is revealed, while so much else remains forever hidden.

I forgot Lola with surprising ease, for from the moment I stopped seeing her she ceased to exist for me and she might just as well never have existed, even though it was with her that I committed the most serious of all my sins. Yet my conscience cannot have been very developed, because it was many years before I felt any remorse for my behaviour.

A more passionate boy would have had different reactions, but mine was a very strange temperament, one moment warm, the next cold, and I was unaware of my true nature. The evening before I left Genoa, my brother-in-law took me to the opera to see *La Bohème*. His choice seemed to me to stem from a very basic intelligence and I secretly despised this man, just as I despised so many others while appearing to be quiet and kindly. So I listened politely. We went outside at the interval. It was a warm evening and some prostitutes were walking slowly up and down in front of the theatre. My brother-in-law winked at me, and just as one of these women passed by he said, 'Good evening, Mimi.' (Mimi as in *La Bohème*). He must know her, I thought naively. Then it suddenly crossed my mind that he may have guessed that I was a virgin and wanted to provide me with the opportunity to be one no longer. My mind working with unaccustomed speed, I reckoned that it was not by chance that I had been left alone with Lola. The intuition was so strong that I cannot rule it out even today. Is it possible that he arranged it all? I can only pose the question. In any case, I pretended not to notice that the streetwalker was desperately giving me the eye. The thought of my Uncle Willie probably came to my mind. I didn't want to end up like him. With a faun's smile and his habitual slight stutter, my brother-in-law eventually said that it was time to return to our seats if we wanted to see Mimi, the real one, cough herself to death.

What a strange man he was! As I grew up he always treated me with great politeness. He no longer made fun of my face, nor had any reason to correct my English, but I now believe that he may have thought my prolonged innocence was not very sensible and that he would have liked to push me discreetly into a woman's arms. I did not understand, and besides, I believed that all street women were infected with the germs of a disease that I didn't even want to name — my uncle's disease.

Did I say my prayers? Did I go to Mass? Did I read the Bible? I cannot answer any of these questions with any certainty. I have forgotten. When I returned to Roncade, spring was bursting out all over the Veneto, the trees and bushes were turning to green, the air was warm, and at night one could hear the cicadas singing. A wind of happiness seemed to breathe over this corner of the world and I had a share of it. Every hour brought some joy and I would sing as I walked along the roads. But what did I sing? How could I forget? Those old Catholic hymns which once so entranced me at the Rue Cortambert, the *Jesu dulcis memoria*, and no doubt, the Protestant psalms and hymns which my mother used to sing in her quavering voice, tapping out the rhythm with her foot. I prided myself on singing correctly and even rather well. Did I not do everything rather well? I was extremely vain, and it was a fault that seemed to be increasing, yet it is nevertheless true to say that I sang hymns and psalms.

I have omitted to mention that on my return from Genoa I arrived at Mestre station in the middle of the night and was obliged to wait until the next morning for a bus to take me to Roncade. Not knowing what to do with my time, I stretched out on one of the wooden benches in the station, covered myself with my great-coat and fell into a very deep sleep. When I awoke, I heard a station employee laughing and asking me if I had slept well. 'Yes, I did . . . ' — 'But didn't you hear anything?' — 'No, nothing'. He told me that Austrian planes had tried to destroy the station during the night but had only succeeded in bombing the railway line about thirty metres away. Yet I had never slept better. It is no exaggeration to say that the explosions could not have woken me.

That sense of *joie de vivre*, of zest for life, did I ever feel it more strongly than I did in April and May of 1918? There was a war. There was nothing I could do about it. The sense of pure happiness used to make me laugh out loud. I would get over-excited by some of the bad books I read but I don't think I lapsed into impure acts. On this point my memory does not deceive me. It seems to me that everything occurred in my mind, though it was no less dangerous for that. I remember deliberately sitting down at my table one day in order to write pages of pathological obscenity. Only one sentence from the story has remained in my mind. This sentence had nothing to do with any book I had ever read and I don't know how I suddenly came to write it, but it flowed so well, was so full of meaning and seemed to me so well expressed that I burst out laughing. I ran to look at myself in the mirror and touched my face; I saw there was not a single hair on my chin,I was as smooth as the statues in the museums and I repeated my sentence while watching the movement of my lips: that was how these words should be said, the mouth should be formed in just such a way. I had never said things of this kind, and I had the impression that as my words broke the silence they echoed around my head. And where had I heard these words which I thought I had put together so cleverly? At the lycée, I expect. I felt myself overcome with a sort of intoxication. With words I could do what others were unable to do. I wrote sentences and something sprang to life around me. In my solitude, Mr Kreyer's magic library seemed to come alive, but it was no longer a question of drawings on paper: there was blood flowing beneath the skin, the flesh lived. In a flash, the hallucinations of my sixth year came back to me and evil stole through my mind as if it had rediscovered a route through the corridors of a palace. I doubt if there was a more decisive moment in my life. I did not abandon myself to any of the actions one might have expected. The terrifying joy remained within me.

I had the feeling that day, that in writing out this sentence I had spoken, someone stronger than me was guiding my hand, yet I was not afraid. Quite the contrary, I rejoiced, and experienced that mysterious satisfaction which the sense of power can bring. So many years later, I can see myself again, sitting at the table and laughing to myself. Had I known what was happening to me, I would have dropped to my knees, but there was no question of that. I had become a pagan again.

Back at Roncade, in the house I shared with five or six

others, there had been some small changes during my absence. I was still on my own in the same bedroom, but the room which was on the other side of the gallery (it was too spacious to be called a corridor) was now occupied not just by two men, but three, which made it look rather congested. There was an explanation for this but I was never told. The new arrival was called Jack and I knew almost immediately that he was the son of a Presbyterian minister.

Although he was a whole year younger than me, he was much taller, and I was immediately struck by the exceptional beauty of his body which one sensed beneath his clothing. It occurred to me later that his long legs could only be compared to those of some of the students at the military school at Fontainebleau, so elegant and strong were they. His robust yet slender figure commanded admiration and if his head had been slightly larger he would have been physically perfect. His dark blond hair covered his forehead leaving only a sort of white diadem to crown his pink angel's face and generous lips. So much for his positive features. The dark side of the picture, at least for me, was that this boy, who appeared to have left his wings in some cupboard, could only express himself in the most disgusting way. He swore obscenely at every opportunity and I realize today that he must have been at least as innocent as me, for his scatology was of the type used only by very small children. I don't know what he can have been trying to rid himself of by speaking like this — only a psychologist would know — but when I listened to Jack, his foul invective would conjure up such images in my mind that I could not bear it any longer and so I would try to avoid him. He was charming yet hateful. He was certainly a curious case. One day, however, something happened. I was alone with him in his room. He was sitting on his camp bed which had been placed sideways across the room and he was reading from a small black book. Seeing me, he got up. I am not sure whether he particularly liked me. He knew, in fact, that I was a Catholic, one of that strange breed. Furthermore, I happened to be from the South, while he, like every other boy in the section, was from the North. All Yankees, except me. I asked him what he was reading and he showed me the cover of the book on which there was writing I did not recognize. '*Hé kainé diathéké*,' he announced in a strident, rather nasal voice. And opening the book, he continued: '*To kata Mathaïon éouanghélion.*' (At least that is what I suppose, for he was reading from the beginning.) I said nothing and he could see that I did not understand. 'The Gospel of Our Lord Jesus Christ', he said in English.

'You read Greek, Jack?'

'Just like English. My father taught me.'

'Can you open that book anywhere and read it just as if you were reading English?'

Each time he replied, he would read a few verses from the Gospel in English, then he would show me the book like a conjuror displaying his cards, as if to prove to me that he was not using any translation. I must have stood with my mouth agape, I was so astonished. 'An angel', I thought, stepping back a pace.

I said nothing more to him that day and returned to my room in silence. If only I could remember what passed through my mind then, but apart from what I have just described it has all vanished.

Nevertheless, there was another day. Having risen early as usual, I saw that Jack's door was open and I thought I would peep into his room. He was in there on his own, asleep. His room-mates were washing, but since Jack swore obscenely when he was woken too early, he would wash after everyone else. As I stood in the doorway, not moving, my heart was beating furiously. What strange urge was it that made me want to lean over the slumbering figure and lay my face on his cheek which sleep had made even pinker than usual? With his golden locks spread over the pillow and the powerful outline of his long sinuous body, he looked so handsome that I was overcome with a joy that was mixed with fear, though I could explain neither the joy nor the fear. He was certainly better looking than me, but then he was blond. I admired him with all my heart. I was not troubled by any wicked thoughts, but I did have to make an enormous effort to pull myself away from this room and leave the house. I was still unfamiliar with the frenzy that sensual feelings can arouse, for I had an overriding distaste for such matters. Later, there would be a lot to overcome. For me, humanity's shame consisted in those parts of the body immediately beneath the stomach, and I tried to pretend they did not exist, yet the beauty of a human face overwhelmed me. I did not realize either that I was probably in love with Jack and that it was only his foul language that had cured me of my passion, though that morning he said not a word, lying open to my gaze and to a chaste yet burning desire which I did not begin to understand. For several minutes I must have suffered, and suffered greatly, for I did not know what it was I wanted; whatever it was tortured me and made me feel like rolling about on the ground.

From that moment until I left the Veneto, I don't think I said more than four words to the boy. Perhaps we shook hands on the last day, but I never saw him again and, as Pascal would say, that was it, forever.

Three months later, on the French front, Jack's jaw was blown away by an exploding shell.

Shortly after I returned from Genoa, a priest, a little Italian chaplain in uniform, called to see me in my room. I don't know why he wanted to see me. All I know is that we stood by the open window speaking and that before he left he gave me two pamphlets, one of which was called *Confessatevi!*, and the other, *Communicatevi!* I leafed through a few pages and put them aside. They did not make much sense to me in my present frame of mind.

I was struck, however, by something I heard one day when two of my colleagues were discussing their leave, which they had spent in Rome. One of them had been to St Peter's. He was a Protestant. All the rich finery appeared barbaric and unchristian to him, for, to his way of thinking, the incense and hymns affected one's feelings, not one's heart or soul. I was used to these objections, and at any other time I would have responded, but I waited for what came next. 'There were lots of people gathered around a confessional, each one of them waiting their turn. As one came out, his or her place would be taken by another. Suddenly, I saw Lodge coming out from behind the curtain.' Lodge was a big boy who wore glasses. He was the quietest person in our section and I had never said more than a word or two to him. The story interested me. 'Old chap, you would never have recognized him! He walked past me without seeing me and his face was radiant with joy.'

What he said gave me quite a shock and, without making a sound, I got up and left. Why not admit what I thought? I felt frightfully jealous of Lodge, the Catholic. Envious would be the more exact word. Not envious in a praiseworthy way, but wretchedly envious like a child who sees someone else with something he wants. I too wanted that wonderful peace which confession brings, but without giving up anything. Giving up what? Sensuality? It wasn't something I knew about. The desire for sensuality then, for everything the devil filled my heart with. I wanted everything, heaven and earth, at once. My soul yearned for all possible goodness and in spite of everything I think it would not have been too difficult to speak to this unhappy soul, if there had been someone ready to do so. The Italian chaplain never realized, and restricted himself to leaving me some pamphlets. No doubt the grumpy chaplain from Monastier-di-Treviso would have found the necessary words, but, in fact, although I lived in total solitude so far as religion was concerned, a single phrase was all that would have been needed to break the magic circle that had formed around me.

It has to be said that my natural unsociability did not help. When I was in a good mood, everyone smiled at me, but I would often shut myself up in my room and would not mix easily with the others in our group. My abruptness was disconcerting. One day a friend asked if he could borrow a silver watch which meant a lot to me. The next day he came to find me. He had the watch in his hand.

'I don't know what's the matter. It's not working.'

I was sitting at my table. 'Give me the watch.'

I took it, looked at it and with a sudden gesture, threw it out of the window. 'You've broken it, I don't want it any more.'

My friend gaped in astonishment and disappeared.

I sometimes had occasion to go to a small town by the name of Mogliano, which was always full of soldiers, and one day I recognized a lieutenant who had worked in my father's office before the war. He was a Venetian and he would have struck me as being very handsome if only he did not have bags under his eyes. I imagined that he had just been sleeping with a woman and so I rather envied him, even though tumescence seemed to me to be a punishment from heaven, rather like the dark circles I once had under my eyes. He spoke to me in a friendly but hurried way, as if he did not really want to be chatting to me and had other things to do, I said to myself under my breath, such as returning to that woman. I wanted him to introduce me to her and in the course of a few seconds I imagined a thousand delightful but impossible things. I felt terribly disappointed when he left me in the middle of the street.

In this same town where I used to wander around and where my uniform attracted many a gaze, I had often noticed a young soldier with a wonderful face who was nearly always to be seen with a young woman as pretty as he was handsome. Looking at them gave me an intense pleasure, but it was not sensual, for I did not really know anything of the power of the flesh yet, except in an abstract way picked up in French novels or from vague dreams, and what was strange in my case was that whenever I found myself face to face with someone I might have desired, my imagination stopped working. In any case, the two young people soon became aware that I was staring at them and asked me to join them for a cup of coffee.

There I was, a moment later, sitting opposite this man and this woman at a long table. I can see it all again quite clearly. Sitting with my back to the sun, I looked at them admiringly while they, elbows on the table and shoulders touching, leaned towards me so closely that our faces almost touched. How white their teeth were and how their eyes shone! 'Do you like us?' asked the soldier, and with a blush, I answered that I did. While he spoke of other things that I have forgotten, the *signorina* gave me a flashing smile, and it suddenly occurred to me that they were lovers. I experienced a strange thrill when, with a flash of intuition, I realized that they wanted me to share their pleasures. From that moment on, I only ever saw them as one person. In fact, they looked like brother and sister, and I was overcome with an anxiety I cannot describe, in which fear and joy were mixed in equal proportions. It was then that the soldier did something I did not understand. They both winked at each other, then he laughed and said to me: 'You know, she and I, we're engaged'. Later, I realized this was a joke, but at the time, I took this expression literally and almost instantly a barrier was formed between this couple and myself. I believed that in a kind way they were reproaching me for having stared at them as I did and I felt guilty. The word adultery came to mind. Thanking the boy and girl for their kindness, I got up and left. I never went back to Mogliano again. The extraordinary thing about this story is that I forgot these lovers almost immediately; it was only many years later that the memory of their wonderfully dark, laughing and watchful eyes came back to me. The chance had been lost.

Some time later, on a bright and warm afternoon, five or six of my colleagues asked me to join them for a short walk along the canals which stretched out to the middle of the fields. I could not have conceived of a more charming landscape. The lines of trees were reflected in the still water and we sat down on the grass to chat. Someone suggested swimming in the canal and the idea was welcomed by everyone except me for I could not swim. 'That doesn't matter', they said as they were undressing. 'Take off your clothes and you can paddle in the water.' I did not want to look like a spoil-sport so I obeyed and a moment later I was standing naked on the grass a little way away from my colleagues who were all watching me. Without knowing why, I felt terribly ashamed. I avoided looking in their direction because they were naked, but I could feel them staring at my body and eventually I said, 'Why don't you go for a swim?' At that moment one of them got up and walked a few paces towards me. He was very blond, with a hooked nose, and in my mind I compared him to a golden crow. When I saw that he had moved very close to me, I stepped away quickly, for he was holding out his hand and I thought he was going to touch me. I realized then that the reason they had made me undress was to see what I looked like and I blushed with embarrassment. 'You shouldn't feel ashamed,' said the boy with a smile. 'You're built like a boxer.'

If he meant that as a compliment, it gave me no pleasure, for according to the values I held at that time, a boxer represented just about the lowest rung on the ladder of human achievement. There was a silence, then the boys jumped into the water, laughing, and I went in myself, feeling rather humiliated. I was in a hurry for the bathing to finish. I noticed that in spite of myself everything about these bodies created a revulsion in me that I could not explain. One should not go around naked, or stare at each other, or pass by so closely that our bodies almost touched. All that was wrong. I stepped out of the water, and after drying in the sun, I put on my clothes as quickly as possible. Once dressed, everything returned to normal. I could now chat to my colleagues again — and recognize them again — for their nudity produced the same effect in me as that on domestic animals when they see their master getting into a bath. Gustave Doré's characters belonged to a different world, as did those of Albano and Giulio Romano. A distinction was beginning to form in my mind that I would have found difficult to put more clearly.

A few days later, I was in another boy's room, and I remember sitting near a window through which a beam of light shone and noticing a book entitled *Three Weeks*. Several of my friends were there, laughing and gossiping, and I asked them what *Three Weeks* was like. 'It's a book they read in brothels', said one of them. I hesitated a moment, then opened it at random, feeling a little anxious for I knew I was doing something wrong. My eyes fell on an apparently anodine phrase, but one which has lodged itself in my memory for good. I didn't understand it very well; frankly, I didn't understand it at all, but it came back to me later laden with meaning and with poison. With an uncontrolled gesture which was made in spite of myself, as if I had been commanded to do so, I closed the book and never opened it again. This small incident strikes me as more mysterious than many acts in the spiritual plain which might appear more important.

There is another recollection which tells me what I must have been like at the time. In our section there was tall boy who was interested in the occult. His unprepossessing physique and the jolly yet condescending manner in which he spoke to everybody except me, exasperated everyone else. The day came when they decided to organize a small ceremony and chuck him in the canal. I had nothing against the boy, but out of cowardice I took part in this nasty little ritual. It took place at night. The victim was pulled out of his bed and put on a stretcher which was carried as far as one of the canals behind the house. Eight or ten of the boys then began chanting as if it were a burial, and here is the ignominious detail: one of them gave me a book and said: 'Here, you're the one who is going to become a priest'. I laughed, took the book and almost at once threw it on the grass, but I had not refused to take it, and I remember that despite my laugh, which was a laugh of embarrassment, I had severe pangs of conscience. I had taken no pleasure in seeing the boy thrown in the water (the stretcher was returned later) and, back in my room and on my own, my cheeks and forehead were burning. I could not forget the words which bothered me more than anything else: 'You're the one who is going to become a priest'. They must have known something. Had I told them about my vocation? I can't remember. Only the bare facts remain.

For the first time in my life I felt ashamed to be myself. The next day, I went to look for the victim. I can see the scene very well. The poor boy had snake-like eyes which, of course, he could not help, but deep down I despised him for being so ugly. Those snake eyes looked at me so reproach-fully. 'You were with them', he said. I told him I was sorry for what had happened.

A week or ten days later something much more serious took place. Among us there was a Frenchman of about thirty whom we nicknamed, I am not sure why, the Count. Small, thin and very talkative, he dazzled my rather naïve col-leagues with the speed of his repartee; he knew all there was to know, he had read everything, and he had a habit of making dogmatic statements about people, about countries and about the war. I had very little to do with him but, when the opportunity arose, I used to try to engage him in conversation just for the pleasure of speaking French. One day when I was telling him that I had enjoyed reading *La Guerre en Dentelles* by Georges d'Esparbes, he replied in a rather superior way, 'A hundred pages of Georges d'Esparbes are not worth one of Anatole France.' I didn't argue, I kept quiet and went away. It seemed clear that I was of no interest to him.

He was much more interested in certain ambulance drivers in our section, and in one especially, a splendidly built boy by the name of Jeffries who, in everyone's opinion, would have been perfect if only the space between his eyes were a little wider. I can see him still with his triumphant gait, his high and mighty tone, so aware of his charm. One evening while he and I and a few others were waiting for dinner, I heard him giving precise and revolting details, accompanied by laughs of mockery and embarrassment, of a story which horrified me, but which I nevertheless listened to very attentively. The evening before, yielding to the Count's pressing entreaties, he had given him what he wanted so badly. In this way I learned how *that* was sometimes done and I immediately conceived a violent and extreme disgust for the act. The account, which was greeted with much mirth, was related in a tone of indignation which may or may not have been sincere, for it seemed to me that his protests sounded false.

No doubt that would have been the end of the matter had not someone rather more virtuous than the others (for it is true that there is always a traitor somewhere) informed our chief of what he called a shameful disturbance. Unfortunately for the Count, American army officers arrived the day after this incident in order to check everyone's military status. Actually, they were looking for shirkers and everyone was aware that a number of young men of call-up age had taken shelter in the Red Cross organizations in the hope of avoiding unnecessary danger while they waited for hostilities to cease.

We all assembled in the marble-tiled dining-room. The table had been pushed against the wall — in such a way as to create the necessary space for a stage set which would help to fix the unforgettable drama in our memories. All the men in the section were gathered at one end of the room, while one of the officers took his place at a small table some way from us and proceeded to open his notebook. He was a cold and rather unpleasant looking man, strapped so tightly into his uniform that there were gaping holes between the buttons.

One after the other, we were summoned into the room, took a few steps in his direction and saluted. In my case, as I had not yet reached the required age to serve in the army, I was dismissed with a wave, but others were told to return to Paris and report to the American military authorities. There were some worried faces and our chief who was standing next to the officer was sweating profusely, knowing all too well what was going to happen.

Then it was the turn of the Count. From the anguished expression on our chief's face, I realized that he must have told the truth about the 'shameful disturbance'. Why? Had they threatened him with revealing everything if he did not admit to his relationship, and if so, how would they punish him? He was not a bad man, but he was weak and suffered from depression.

There was a deep silence when the Frenchman stepped forward. I noticed that his face had turned grey as if all his blood had been drained out of it. In a low and tremulous voice, the officer asked him why he was not serving his own country's army, and the Count, sounding really rather feeble, muttered something about his health.

Raising himself a little in his chair, the officer then began to insult him in a furious outburst that set my heart beating. There were words that I had never heard before, but whose meaning I guessed immediately, and they echoed like the cries of an animal in the ghastly silence, for there was something beyond anger in all this rage. The man had so much to say about the scandalous behaviour that he seemed to be gasping for breath. It took years for me to realize that a great deal of his fury consisted of envy and that he was releasing his own accumulated lust by shouting like this. His frustration was obvious. Without realizing it, he betrayed himself by acquitting Jeffries whose blushing cheeks made his beauty shine even more than usual. The trial ended on a sentence which hit us like a bullet: 'You will return home', he shouted at the accused, 'and I hope that you will be sent to the front where you will find what you deserve.'

For all of us at the time, the word 'front' was synonymous with death, and for a moment we stood speechless and motionless, like figures in a wax museum. As for the Count, he appeared to be struck rigid with terror and one of us had to nudge his arm to tell him to go back to his place. His half-open mouth did not utter a sound. Where was all that loquacity, the mockery, the witty retorts? Condemned and trying to come to terms with his verdict, he spoke not a word. We never saw him again. That very evening a car arrived to take him to Padua station.

Did the story end there? Not quite. The next day, by a stroke of bad luck, which I have good reason to think was inspired by the Devil, I sat next to Jeffries in the ambulance which he was driving to I forget which advance first-aid post. The 'victim' of the foreign seducer cut a rather curious figure. I don't know what was going though his mind or his conscience, but he kept his teeth clenched firmly throughout the entire journey. As for me, I could hardly keep still. Something was troubling me which I couldn't understand. Certain aspects of the Jeffries story struck me as pretty squalid, but in spite of that I still wanted to speak to him. For the first time in my life I could sense the presence of evil, and by tempting me with evil, the Devil crept into my soul, not through love — there was no question of that — but through vice, which frightened me as much as it fascinated me. I was sitting beside a man who had done wrong, though he was no less handsome in my eyes, yet he terrified me so much that it was as if the Devil himself had taken possession of his face, his features, his whole body. Feeling as if someone were trying to strangle me, I attempted to press myself ever so slightly against him, but he pushed me back roughly with his elbow. This strange pantomime continued for a while until, weary and confused, I eventually moved away from my companion.

I do not mean to romanticize my account or let anyone think that I was not fully aware of the fate that would await me in Hell if I lost control of myself, but I do know that that afternoon on a road in the Veneto, I suddenly had the feeling that I was prey to something which I could not see. Through some trick of the memory I remembered, as if I had been prompted, that my cousin Sarah had once mentioned Jeffries' name to me and that he must have visited our home when I was in the Argonne. After much hesitation, I asked Jeffries whether he knew my cousin. He glanced at me and nodded; that was all. Anyone else would have known how to carry on this slight attempt at a conversation, but I could only feel rejected. It was clear that I was of no interest to my companion. I was a child. My efforts had obviously been in vain. I don't know what happened after that. Years later, I learned that Jeffries had been killed at the front. His voice, his face, his whole personality came back to me and he stood before me like a ghost. I felt a surge of affection for this apparition. Pity made me see him as soul tormented by the memory of betrayal, but how can one even begin to make sense of such things?

Life went on. One day, our commanding officer announced that three boys who had spent the day in Venice without leave were to be sent home. One of them was James, the boy who was in love. He came up to me and said, 'Greeno (that was what they called me), the chief wants to get rid of us. Are you staying?' 'No', I said rashly and without thinking, 'if you are being sent back then I'm going too.' Why did I say that? There was no doubt that I felt injustice had been done, but what a strange way of making one's protest. . . The departure of those who were guilty would not really have bothered me. In any case, they did not leave. Our chief must have had a sleepless night, for by the next day he had changed his mind.

I had signed on for six months and I had now come to the end of my commission. I was asked where I wanted to go. I said Rome and so they gave me a ticket to Rome as a present.

Before leaving Roncade I had a few more discussions with James about his unhappy love affair which I could not take seriously since, as I kept telling him, it concerned a man. This was heartless of me as well as forgetful, for surely I still remembered my schoolfriend Frédéric in Paris? On the other hand, strange as it may seem, I never thought of myself as being in love, precisely because I did not realize that love could exist between people of the same sex — nor knew what name to give to the feelings I had had for the boy at the lycée — and I also have to admit that both James and the boy he longed for struck me as being so ugly that I was not interested in their affair. No doubt I would have paid more attention had either of them been handsome, but because of their unfortunate looks I did not bother. Alas! I used to laugh at him, never realizing that one day I would pay for such laughter with a good many tears.

So it was that I arrived in Rome at the beginning of June 1918 and immediately went to the Elysée Hotel where my sister Mary had rooms. Had she changed? Not at all. She seemed in good health; still the same voice, the same good natured manner that struck us as being simultaneously imperious and persuasive. She was usually surrounded by Italian, Belgian or French friends, among whom I always felt ill at ease, for they lived in a world of their own, with their own language, their own jokes and innuendo which I did not begin to understand. If the truth be known, I was a bit scared of the slightly unpleasant way they looked at me. I had no idea how to converse wittily. With a great sweep of her hand, my sister pointed to the window from which there was a fine view of St Peter's. As if in a dream, I saw the distant dome standing out against a cloudless sky for the first time, and I felt a surge of profound joy, tinged at the same time with a touch of mistrust. The joy was Catholic, but I don't know what brought about the mistrust unless it was some Protestant atavism. In any case, I stood there speechless. What can one possibly say about St Peter's if one is surrounded by rather sophisticated Italians? Some frivolous remarks were made which shocked me deeply, for this, after all, was St Peter's, it was the Faith. But at that very moment I felt as if some gift had been bestowed on me. It was like the solution to a private debate. It suddenly no longer mattered to me what was said by others, for I was proud to be a Catholic and I thanked God with all my heart; there was no longer any of that shameful distrust, suddenly everything within me said yes; confused, muddled, but joyful, it was my first prayer. It seemed to me that anything that had been taken from me at any previous time was now being restored to me in a spirit of gaiety — yes, a divine gaiety which made everything glow with happiness in the most beautiful light in the world. I would go so far as to say that I had the sense of being made welcome. Had I been alone, I would have knelt down, but I was surrounded by sophisticated, witty people for whom such matters had no meaning, and that sense of wonderment was soon followed by feelings of sadness and guilt.

I find it somewhat difficult to write about what follows next. The artificial luxury of hotel life was something completely new to me. At our home in Paris everything had seemed straightforward and clear-cut. Here, I was very aware of the fur rugs on the sofa and the brocade cushions, and details like these made me almost as shy as did the conversation and the smiles, for one had to smile at all costs in order to be amusing. There were endless stories about people I did not know whose voices and mannerisms they would imitate. It amused them to refer to me as a 'soldier' and then, having offered me coffee in a tiny gold cup, they would totally forget I was there (which delighted me) and proceed to discuss the latest book just published in Rome: *Quaresimale*. The title suddenly comes back to me. Everybody, including my sister, spoke Italian so quickly that I hardly understood a word. I noticed a wooden rosary lying on the edge of a table, which I supposed must have belonged to Mary, and I felt reassured. At least she was a believer. It was essential to believe. Poor Mary! She seemed to think that by showing me the dome of St Peter's with her grand gesture she was making a present of the whole city to me, for there was no question of being shown anything else that day.

Actually, the room with the fine view of St Peter's was not in my sister's apartment, but in one belonging to a young man, an actor whom I shall call Giulio. Every day we would gather at his home for coffee. He was generally considered to be handsome, although I did not think so, for if his eyes were a magnificent blue, the rest of his face and what one glimpsed of his body did not seem to me to correspond to the Greek ideal, beyond which, according to the way I thought at the time, there was no aesthetic salvation. Naturally, I kept these opinions to myself. Giulio's plumpness was something I found horrifying in a man. Everyone knew he had particular tastes, except for me for whom such things were meaningless. The man he lived with was also present at these gatherings. He is dead now. I shall call him Enzio and I cannot think of him without regret, for I have rarely known an Italian who was more serious-minded, more refined or, in his own way, more Christian. He may have been forty years' old, whereas Giulio could scarcely have been more than twenty, and there was a world of difference between them. No two people could have been more dissimilar and when their true relationship was revealed to me, five or six years later, I found it hard to believe. Enzio would look at me solemnly and would occasionally speak to me in his marvellously deep and sweet voice. His emaciated face, with features so fine they might have been drawn by pencil, could have been that of a priest. I never knew what to say to him, but I liked his quiet manner whereas I was frightened by Giulio's rather irreverent teasing.

In addition to these two, there were two charming Belgians, who I had better not mention in case they recognize themselves, and a woman, also Belgian, accompanied by her son who had a habit of twitching which I often felt I wanted to imitate. That is all I recall of this small world which was certainly colourful but not one in which I felt particularly comfortable.

Also present was my sister Anne who said very little. She had left the Ritz Hospital after Retta's death in order to look after Mary whose health so concerned my father, but since she was short of money, she worked for part of each day at the American Red Cross. She had been deeply affected by everything she had been through in Paris, but she was in the full bloom of her beauty at the time and never said a word about many things which must have appalled her. I saw very little of her. Basically, they didn't really know what to do with me. Someone who doesn't say anything can be a nuisance. On the third day, I left the hotel in the morning and rushed out into the street. Hailing a hackney cab, I asked the *vetturino* to take me to the Jesuit church, the celebrated 'Il Gesù', so well-known for the sumptuousness of its interior and its unique *trompe l'oeil* vault. Unfortunately, I could not make myself understood to the *vetturino* and kept yelling 'Gesù' at him in vain. He must have taken me for a religious fanatic, for eventually, with a shrug of his shoulders, he flicked his whip and the horse trotted off.

In giving this short account, I do recall that I wanted to go to church and that I considered myself to be in a suitable state for the transmission of grace. The thought that I was living in Rome meant a great deal to me. I say all this with a touch of melancholy.

One night, just as I was going to bed, I heard noises in the room next to mine that should have left me in no doubt as to what was going on. I can see myself standing with my ear glued to a door which must have seemed as thin as a sheet of paper to a boy whose hearing was as sharp as mine. For a second or two, I thought that my neighbours must have been ill, but it was hardly a question of that! Pain had little to do with this groaning and very soon the crudeness of the words they mumbled removed any doubt.

I don't remember which writer it was who said that in a similar situation one sees with one's ears. With my head aflame, but my body completely calm (will I ever understand this mystery?),in my imagination I took part in this unknown act which I found both terrifying and fascinating, and to which I attributed every possible virtue. That was it, that was what I wanted more than anything else in the world at that moment. Not knowing what to do, and forgetting I was almost naked, I rushed to the door of my room and noted the kind of shoes that were placed for cleaning so carefully outside the door of the adjoining room. When I say shoes, I am not being accurate: there were a pair of officer's boots and a pair of lady's slippers, and they looked so innocent and ordinary that if I had not been beside myself with excitement, I would have burst out laughing. But the most extraordinary part of this story is that having returned to my room, I forbade myself to listen further, and once I was back in bed I fell asleep immediately.

Next day, when I was having breakfast in the dining-room with Mouser, our old English friend who also lived at the hotel, I looked carefully at everyone's feet as they came in. There were countless numbers of boots and all the ladies shoes looked strangely alike. I was expecting to see Phoebus and Aphrodite arrive, wearing *my* boots and *my* slippers, but there were only dumpy men and plain women, and I spent so much time staring at all these feet that eventually Mouser began to wonder if I had lost anything. I blushed. If she had known. . . But if she had known she would have laughed till she cried. . .

It is time I spoke about dear old Mouser, a chip off the old block of that stubborn Albion we find so hard to understand. Her real name was Florence Carew-Gibson. My father, who had a terrible memory, would invariably call her Mrs Webster, and I have no idea where the nickname Mouser came from. In English, Mouser is the name given to cats that catch mice, but there was nothing feline about Mouser. She had a rather rugged face, lined by life's troubles, somewhat manly features and a fixed look in her eyes, which rarely blinked except from the smoke of her cigarette which she never put out. Protestant to the marrow of her bones, she would speak about Catholics with such respect and diplomacy that she must have been very solidly anti-papist. Her way of dressing was proverbial in our family. Chains, rings, precious stones, cameos, feathers and lace did their best to improve all that was humdrum about contemporary taste, adorning features that she was the first to admit were not getting any prettier, and the prospect of old age filled her with mounting horror. Her very precise and cutting manner of speaking made her conversation somewhat alarming, for sarcasm flowed from her narrow lips, but it was a sarcasm mingled with politeness and a natural kindness which she probably regarded as uncontrollable weakness. Tough though she wanted herself to appear, she could not be other than kind. She was well respected. She just needed to be loved. Nevertheless, she knew that in our rather appalled way we were fond of her and it meant a lot to her. Disregarding the fact that we were not British, which was bad enough, she took each one of us into her guarded fortress of a heart. We were, after all, of English descent and at least we didn't speak like Americans. When I was still a child, I used to write to her from Paris when she was in Italy with Mary, and I signed my letters, 'Your respectable friend', thinking that I had written, 'Your respectful friend'. She was delighted by the mistake. Much later, when I was twenty and — as she supposed without any disapproval — spending most of my time in female company, she would write to me occasionally and would sign off, 'Your one respectable friend'. The news of my conversion in 1916 must have caused her to raise her eyebrows disdainfully, but Mary had done the same, and Eleonore before her. Was this the influence of the underworld on a spineless family? She was certainly true to her word. If anyone had spoken to her about the dangers of being tainted by Catholicism in a city like Rome, she would have removed her silver-framed lorgnette so as to laugh the louder. She did not despise us, however. There was a quality of stubbornness in our family which she respected and once, when some of us were trying to resolve a difficult piece of homework, she looked at us and let fall the word 'thoroughbreds'. She often used horsy terms (she rode as a girl) and, coming from her, it was no small compliment. She was married once, then separated but never divorced, and sometimes she would make vitriolic references to this husband whom she only ever called 'mister' with an alarming, silent kind of chuckle. Proud of bearing, despite being racked by rheumatism, with her manly, quiet authority, she became part of our lives. I never cared for her in the way I once did for my good, plump, wicked godmother, Agnes, but I was fond of her and I admired her. She always addressed me with that faint note of respect which, despite everything, she reserved for the male sex, keeping her most disdainful darts for women, yet, ever so politely, she dominated me. The Italians struck her as comic and charming, rather like monkeys in their habits and intelligence. By some curious British paradox, she could not stand her compatriots, even though she realized that between them and the rest of the world there was roughly the same difference as between man and the animal kingdom. But like many English people, she preferred to live among the apes rather than in her own country, for the apes were more amusing.

I can see now that there were two conflicting forces in my life then, and that one kept the other in check. Mary did not feel strong enough to join me in the dining-room, which is why I took my meals with Mouser. One day, Mouser told me that an Italian officer's son would be joining us at table and, sure enough, a boy of about my own age, elegantly dressed in a navy blue suit, sat down opposite me. At first, I was not particularly struck by his looks, except for noticing a certain gaiety and something verging on impatience about him, but he was polite and had good manners. After a while, however, I became aware of just how handsome he was with his beautiful skin, white teeth and shiny dark hair. He only knew Italian, but he spoke it with such vivacity that it made me ashamed of how slow I was to express myself in the language; because of this I hardly said a word, but I fear that without my even realizing it, my eyes must have given me away. I remember that Mouser asked the young man how to pronounce the name of the town of Pontedera and whether it should be Pontédera or Ponted-éra. 'Pontédera, *signora*. It's the town where Torquato Tasso spent the summer. And what did he do there? He slept', said the boy with a furtive laugh. Silently, I admired everything he said. Quite simply, I loved him, but it was a totally innocent love and not a single wicked thought crossed my mind. I later discovered that he used to stand at the top of the staircase and pour water over anyone who was coming up; there were complaints and he was punished by his father. Once or twice I came across him again, but after a while I didn't think any more about him.

Since I am mentioning these matters which I did not begin to understand, but which nevertheless caused me some suffering from time to time, I shall say a word about a young officer named Galeazzo who was the object of much admiration on account of his exceptional looks and personality. Even now, I still wonder why such attributes are given to some and not others. If ever I thought that I might possibly be handsome, I only had to look at Lieutenant Galeazzo to hang my head and feel rather humble. I only saw this young man once or twice, and then only for a few minutes. Several years went by before I found myself involved in anything evil, but that's the strange thing about seeds which are planted, develop under the soil and finally germinate.

One morning when I was in my room, someone knocked on my door which had been left ajar and placed a book with a yellow cover on the corner of my bedside table. At the same time I heard Mouser's voice saying to me: 'Good morning. Keep this book. It's obviously written by a madman, but there are some quite amusing passages.' On the cover I read: *Mon Journal*, and above it a name that meant nothing to me: Léon Bloy. To please Mouser, rather than out of curiosity, I flicked through a few pages without finding anything to hold my attention. The general impression I had of the book was that the author was very angry. He either loved the church, or perhaps he hated it. One could not tell exactly, and there were allusions to all sorts of things I knew nothing about. I closed *Mon Journal* and did not look at it again for several months.

My stay in Rome only lasted for three weeks. One evening I was taken to the music-hall where a comedian called Petrolini was enjoying a great success. Everyone was supposed to find him funny but I took a sudden dislike to him, not because of his malicious wit, but because he seemed rather stupid. Enzio, who was very kind, took me to the Forum, and Mouser took me to the Coliseum. Surrounded by all that immense architecture, she seemed to have something else on her mind. In a fit of conscience, she showed me a few churches, such as San Pietro in Vincoli, where Michelangelo's 'Moses' made her smile on account of his horns which are meant to suggest beams of light, but she would always prefer such curious and amusing details, which she could be relied on to discover, rather than the work itself which would often bore her. Her anti-papism did not prevent her from taking me to St Peter's, but perhaps she just wanted to see what effect it would have on me. She walked around with a rebellious air beneath those proud vaults which had so impressed me. I did what my sister had told me, I raised a hand to compare mine to those of the marble cherubs in a chapel. They had seemed so small but I realized they were actually four times the size. Mouser came across a pope with a particularly sinister expression which she drew to my attention, but I was too dumbfounded to listen to what she was saying. I had come ready to admire what I saw and, I suppose, with all kinds of preconceived emotions, but I had no sooner entered the bronze doors than I felt a surge of disappointment. Religion! Where was it? My heart beat anxiously. 'You are at St Peter's', I kept saying to myself, 'at St Peter's in Rome . . .' My mind was in a turmoil as I looked from side to side. Had I been alone, I think I would have fled. It is hard to say this, but I longed for the subtle light of Notre Dame, the towering stonework where the old faith watched over us, but as for praying here — I could not have done so. It would be easy to persuade me that I was wrong and I would readily agree. But I can only say what I felt. I left St Peter's with a heavy heart.

I realize that for many the passage they have just read will give the impression that my attitudes at that time were still those of a Protestant, and that my reactions to triumphal sixteenth-century Rome were not those of a Catholic, which may be true on a purely superficial level. I felt troubled and repelled by this colossal manifestation of power when my only dream was to slip into God's kingdom. Something had been bothering me for a week or ten days and I didn't know what name to give to it. However humble the chapel on the Rue Cortambert may have been, I could not think of it without a great longing to see it again and hear the pure voices of the nuns singing. Nevertheless, I was happy to be in Rome. I admired everything I was told to admire, the amazing height of the vaults, the gold which made the ceilings of the basilicas gleam, all that was exquisite and magnificent, everything. When I left St Peter's with Mouser, she said to me with a smile, 'I will now tell you what one of my friends said after visiting each of the sights of the city: "Well, at least we won't ever have to go there again." ' I could not help laughing, but I kept my thoughts to myself: they would have given too much pleasure to a heretic.

I had been protected from certain dangers, and this stemmed from the fact that I had told everyone that I intended to go into the religious life. Perhaps for this reason, people who might have tried to lead me astray left me alone, for it would have been very easy to kindle in me a fire which was only just dormant and to lead me into evil at an age when I would not have been able to defend myself. Without realizing it, I longed for sensual pleasure. For this reason I was sometimes devastated by sudden attacks of melancholy.

Towards the end of my visit, my sister Mary took it upon herself to take me to some of her favourite churches. She dressed carefully for the occasion and with a charming smile asked me if I was ready. In a flash, seeing her like that, I suddenly found myself transported back to the Rue de Passy (where we used to live), to the sitting room where she played the piano for me, just for me, she would say. Although she was not pretty, she had a particular gracefulness, a way of saying things which always put one in a good mood. We never tired of her company when she had made up her mind to please us and we dreaded those days when, in order to punish us for something we had done, she would tell us that she was not going to speak to us again for a week. (There were, however, truces during those grim weeks when, for example, she could be persuaded by Anne to play cards; then, for about an hour, everything would be normal again, but once the game was finished, she would revert to that awful silence and that blank expression which saw no one). In any case, in Rome she was as delightful as she could be and I shall always remember the afternoon she took me in a hansom to Santa Agnese fuori le Mura. As soon as I entered this ancient and wonderfully beautiful church, I felt transported by a joy which left me speechless. We were surrounded by the countryside and, within these walls, by a silence which seemed to come from the time of the Apostles. It was as if I could touch the Faith itself; it seemed to waft on a breeze, I could breathe it, I wanted to die for it so that I could live forever. This little church, lost amongst the grass and the trees, made up for everything that St Peter's lacked. It must have seen the martyrdom of the early popes and its effect on the visitor was like a still prayer which drew one gently out of this world. This sort of rapture lasted for a few minutes and I came away with regret, sad that one always has to leave, that everything always has to come to an end. Neither Mary nor I spoke for a moment, then words restored the usual banality again, but there had been such a beautiful silence.

Before leaving Rome to go back to Paris, I was careful to visit the photographer in order to preserve a record of my precious countenance. As might have been expected, the photograph made me look like a young Italian. I treasured this slightly absurd portrait. At every possible opportunity, I would remove the print from its envelope to admire it a little more and I had the impression the image improved by the hour. Doubtless, I paled by comparison with Lieutenant Galeazzo, but I reckoned nonetheless that I could look anybody in the face. And what good would that do you, I asked myself. You're not in love with anyone and no one's in love with you. How does one go about finding someone? I remembered wistfully a phrase I had read a year earlier in a book which dealt chastely with what was called the springtime of adolescence: 'How will he resist these urges? Delightful young girls will hover around him . . . ' Not one young girl was hovering around me. Of course there was *la guerre, Madame,* as Géraldy* would say ironically. In my life, the 'fair sex' was represented by our former maid, Mlle Jeanne. She looked nothing like any of the people in the licentious drawings I had seen at Nervi. Something was wrong. I should admit that I did not suffer particularly, for I was as cold as a fish, but just because there was no physical pain it did not prevent my imagination soaring. Everything took place in my head which was now becoming something of a place of ill repute.

* Paul Géraldy, a sentimental but highly successful French poet and writer.(*Tr.*)

Yet, without realizing it, I was changing. When I returned to Paris, I was no longer the same person. My experiences at Santa Agnese, at San Clemente, at the church of Quattro Santi Coronata, had been too powerful for me to view the world in the same way as I had before and gradually a yearning for the unseen took the place of fleshly desire. I discovered a tragic France, with churches full of women in mourning, soldiers in their blue uniforms whom Heaven somehow seemed to have protected. Golden Italy seemed far away. Bitter and grave, the French spoke only of hardship. When I pushed open the door of the chapel near our house, it was as if I was awakening from a long dream. Once again the nuns solemnly sang their beautiful, imperturbable music and I felt I had returned to reality. Religion did not smile here. How could I have ever dreamt of the delights of evil? Austerity can be strangely intoxicating. I began to read the Bible again and became drunk on religion. Since Father Crété was not in Paris, I would go to the convent where I attended Mass with the nuns each morning, and through the thick grills of those dark little visiting rooms, I listened to these women who, dressed in their white serge, looked as souls might have looked. I saw only an eye, a mouth, I heard the rustle of their veils with every movement of their heads, their sensible little laughs, their gentle voices which spoke of my vocation and the poison of the world. My vocation! These words opened a passage to the very depths of my heart.

Our house was a very sad place that summer. My father had not yet come to terms with the death of Retta and he hardly spoke. Only Lucy and I were there to keep him company and Lucy was the most taciturn of the three of us. With her arms folded over her bosom, I never knew what was going on in her poor head. The death of her sister had been such an appalling shock that it affected her physically and she developed a skin complaint which made her suffer terribly, for she thought it would make her ugly forever. Because of this, her head was always sunk over her chest, and whenever she looked up, I was shocked by the distress that could be seen in her large and beautiful green eyes. Sometimes she spoke more gently to me than she would to the others, and I tried to reply to her in the way she wanted, yet confronted by all the suffering she bore, I could find little to say. When she entered a room, it was as if everything darkened because she had become the image of her own sadness, yet there was a violence about her sadness, it was a sorrow combined with a sort of dumb fury. She could not understand her fate. Without a word of bitterness, she rebelled within herself. One day, when she had been studying me rather morosely, she suddenly got up and in a few manly strides left the room saying: 'Boys get everything. It's not fair.' Nevertheless, she loved me and kept photographs of me as well as all my youthful letters to her. I knew that she cried in her loneliness. When she smiled, she looked rather like a tiger trying to be kind, for she was full of love and out of all of us she was perhaps the most tender-hearted. Her life was a mystery whose meaning escapes me and I cannot think about it without some pain, for she suffered and there was no one to console her. She built a wall of silence around her and it seemed impossible to reach her. One day, however — have I mentioned this? — I found a charred piece of paper in the hearth and on one corner which had not been burnt I could read these words in Lucy's handwriting: 'I don't complain, I only observe.' I don't complain . . . Angry words sometimes escaped from her mouth, but she never uttered a single complaint. She read the Bible and her faith remained, in its entirety I think, that of her Protestant mother. My conversion must have upset her. Eventually she came to terms with it and she used to tease me by singing the words of a hymn our parents had taught us:

> The old time religion,
> The old time religion,
> The old time religion
> Was good enough for me!

I can still see her, nodding her head in time to the tune, her hair cut in the style of Joan of Arc, with a spiteful expression on her face as she followed me from room to room, badgering me in that superior manner of hers, and nothing can prevent the stab of pain I feel whenever I think of her.

While she no could no longer look at herself in the mirror without horror and consternation, I would still gaze at myself in admiration, unable to pull myself away from this face which so fascinated me. Religion had not affected it. I looked oddly like the man who has faith but no love, described in St James's epistle, but the difference was that although I had not forgotten what I had seen, I still had to keep on inspecting my face in case I forgot what I looked like. I remember that one day, finding myself alone in the dining-room, I took a silver plate which was on the sideboard and peered at myself with that desperation that I put into everything. Just then I heard someone coming and the fear of being caught unaware made me drop the plate which then rolled on the floor. We still have the plate and it bears the dent marks of that accident in case I should ever forget my incorrigible vanity.

This is the point at which my memory fails me, not for long, it is true, but enough to make me wonder what I did with my time during the weeks following my return from Rome. Clear though the consequences of the intellectual commotion going on within me may be, I have forgotten what was actually happening to me at the time. Facts would remind me, but the facts are missing. All I have to guide me are the signatures and a few dates inscribed in the books I bought at the time. Perhaps they tell me enough. Léon Bloy and Huysmans were my most important acquisitions. I devoured their books. The former fired my mind, the latter filled me with a sad nostalgia for the cloister. There was another book: *Les Heures Bénédictines* by Schneider; written in a somewhat unctuous style, the book seemed to give off an aroma of incense which transported me in the way that Loti's *Les Desenchantées* had done. I made a mental note of this. My notions of sensuality had subtly changed. For the moment, my soul wallowed in sheer delight, convulsed in the sound of church bells or Gregorian chant. It might be said that I speak too lightly about what was probably a divine gift, but the issue at stake is not so much the gift as the way I used it. Everything I did was governed by pride, intense excitement and fanaticism. What should have led me to God separated me instead from humanity. Since I did not fail to let it be known that I planned to withdraw from worldly things in due course (and with a great spiritual fanfare and such luxury of humility . . . I imagined a sort of gala farewell), I would often provoke objections from the Protestant side of the family: unswayable Lucy, and Anne, who was now back from Rome. I would listen patiently, smiling mysteriously and replying very calmly. I was so virtuous. It was at about then that I dropped the silver plate.

At that time, Big Bertha was firing its shells on Paris. On Good Friday of that year, 1918, one had landed on the roof of St Gervais during the afternoon office and some of the congregation had been killed or wounded. Among the dead was a friend of ours, Germaine Francière, who was barely twenty years old. I can't remember why, but my cousin Sarah had to go to the mortuary to identify her. 'She looked totally altered', she wrote to me. The news gave me a shock, which came as an intimation to me once more, but I hardly understood anything about such warnings since, in my own mind, death was something that happened to others and it had orders to spare me.

At home, my father who now returned a little earlier from his office in the Rue du Louvre, paced back and forth from the dining-room to the sitting room, his head down, lost in thoughts which he never spoke about, but which lent him such a sorrowful expression that it was not difficult to guess he was thinking of my mother. Sometimes he smiled at us or asked us questions, or else he would hum some of the tunes from his childhood which would remind us of the American Civil War. I loved him without ever feeling close to him. He always spoke gently to me, but we never had much to say to each other. Lucy, his favourite child, would tease him, speaking to him in that surly voice she always used with us. As for me, I would never have dared to speak to him except in respectful tones. Secretly, what I admired in him was his irreproachable goodness. Neither he nor my mother seemed to me to possess any faults. None of us who had observed them closely with the ruthless eyes of youth could ever discover the least imperfection in either of them. The thought even bothers me now: I had the sort of parents that might have belonged to a saint.

I don't think I mentioned that during a visit he made to the Netherlands in 1916, my father was put to a rather unusual test. I have never been quite sure how it happened, but he was in The Hague on business when he was approached by a German agent. My father was extremely mistrustful of all Germans, and in 1916 they were anathema to him, but the fact is that this particular German had led him to understand that if he agreed to supply Germany with a certain amount of cotton his fortune would be made. As was to be expected, my father refused, but he must have thought long and hard, for his financial position was difficult and his children's futures seemed very uncertain. 'I spent that night pacing up and down my hotel bedroom', he confided in us much later.

I can see him on a fine July afternoon, standing by one of the drawing room windows with his pocket watch in his hand. What can he be waiting for? I don't know, because I'm not sure what time it is. Suddenly, there is an explosion nearby: the shell with which Big Bertha graces us daily at five o'clock every afternoon. This time it fell at the bottom of the Rue Cortambert, in the middle of the Place Possoz. 'By Jove', said my father, replacing his watch in his waistcoat pocket, 'those fellows are remarkable. Never a second late!'

If only he had been younger! I believe I would have been able to speak to him, but he was forty-seven years older than I was. He could have been my grandfather. There was too big an age gap for us to be able to understand each other, and although we loved one another, an intimate relationship was not possible.

I have mentioned my cousin Sarah* before. There can be no doubt that for reasons I could not understand, she was

* See *The Green Paradise*

attractive to men. In fact, she did not seem very pretty to me. Her eyes bulged somewhat and her mouth was almost always half open, but she was certainly not ugly, and her small, slender body did not lack grace. Added to which, she was vivacious in her movements and her expressions; she was gay, cheeky, an amusing gossip, and she was full of heart — too much perhaps. She was extremely proud of her legs, of which she revealed as much as fashion allowed, and it does no discredit to her memory to say that she loved to please. Her visits to our house became increasingly frequent towards the end of the war and, to the despair of my father who would be put to much inconvenience, she would receive her friends in the big drawing room, not allowing them to leave until late at night. A stream of soldiers, sailors, American nurses and de Groslay ladies* would troop into the drawing room where she would serve them refreshments and sweets. Her great talent lay in filling every type of plate (there was a general mobilization of all our crockery on those evenings) with delicious caramels filled with nuts. Where can she have found the necessary sugar and chocolate? There were always some American boys to supply them, a fact that upset our British and French friends who were deprived of most things. One day — how can I ever forget it? — we had a visit from Mrs Maugham, the sister-in-law of the novelist. I am not sure why, but one of us must have suggested putting on a record and so we opened the Victrola gramophone. How shocked and astonished Mrs Maugham was when she realized that the shelves of the gramophone concealed not records, but large plates of caramels, lovingly prepared by our cousin Sarah for what she called one of her parties. Poor Sarah! I

* The de Groslay Institute was a finishing school for young ladies. (*Tr.*)

can see her at the kitchen in the Rue Cortambert, bent over the saucepans she used for making caramel, with her short skirt and her air of mischief, and while she stirred the thick liquid with her wooden spoon, I would watch everything she did, for I was extremely greedy and I knew that eventually I would be given something to lick. Since I was getting on for eighteen (it was after I had returned from Italy) and was almost a man, our would-be cook could not resist paying me compliments.

'Mlle D. said to me the other day that you really weren't at all bad-looking. She spoke to me about your eyes. Personally, I pity the girl who looks into your eyes.'

'Oh? Why?' I asked ponderously.

'Oh! For Heaven's sake, don't be such an ass!'

I knew exactly what she meant and if I played the fool it was only because I was waiting for further compliments; no amount of religion in the world could prevent that. A few moments later, the future anchorite slipped back into his bedroom and examined his eyes as if he had never seen them before. He held the lamp to his face to peer at them from every possible angle. Were they really so fine? I longed to believe so. And did girls really sigh in admiration? Well, well! (I felt rather sorry for them.)

I realize I am only mentioning these foolish things in order to delay writing about Sarah's guests. One of them, the Reverend Guthrie, was a Presbyterian minister who was highly respectable, but young and a bit of a tease. There were also two naval officers, one fat the other thin, who always arrived together and hardly ever spoke to me. There were several others . . . I would make brief appearances during these parties where I would always find a caramel to pilfer.

One day, however, a young American sailor arrived at our home and his visits became more and more frequent, and soon daily. I am not sure what he was doing in Paris, but eventually he moved into our house, and when I went away to Fontainebleau he even slept in my bed. At first, I didn't pay much attention to him. My poor father thought he was a nice boy but too noisy, oh! much too noisy, he would say, blocking his ears. Actually, Ted had a very loud laugh, spoke incessantly and teased everybody, but he was so attractive and so good humoured that it was impossible to feel cross with him. I regarded him rather coolly because I also found him rather noisy and one had to be sensible in this life. His pale gold, tousled hair lent him a sort of glory, to my mind, and his face was almost too handsome, with its upturned nose, deep blue eyes and perfect white teeth. Out of embarrassment, I avoided looking at his fine, muscular neck and the glimpse of his chest of which he seemed rather proud. I was also careful to keep my eyes off his tough and stocky body which was clad, slightly indecently, in a uniform that was too tight. Did Ted deliberately take up poses? Sometimes he would sit straddling the arm of the sofa, or sunk into a big armchair with his legs tucked beneath him, one minute standing, the other sitting on the floor, constantly moving about and bursting out with laughter that could be heard on the street . . .

I was rather shocked by him, but I only had to set eyes on him to experience a powerful tightening feeling inside me. Once he had gone, I forgot all about him, at least to begin with, but later I would cross-question my cousin discreetly. Why? Did I realize? 'Oh, him! He's my favourite!' she told me. 'You must see the nice snapshot he gave me.' She went to find a photograph which I stared at in silence. Why did it affect me so painfully? My cousin asked me whether I liked the look of him. Yes, of course, I thought he looked marvellous.

With the arrival of American youth a lightheartedness was restored to France which we had almost forgotten. All these tall, good-looking young men seemed to be so full of hope. We welcomed them with open arms, even if we cursed them later on when we no longer needed them, but that's another story.

At home, our flat, which I used to think of as such a sad place, now resounded to laughter and our old, slightly out of tune piano, which formerly only ever played tragic nocturnes, now tinkled to the latest jazz tunes. It was the first time that I had ever heard this kind of music and though I found it at once appalling and fascinating, I took a guilty pleasure in listening to it for there was no denying that it was tantalizing. 'The devil take your classical music', said Sarah as she whirled around with her soldiers. 'We want the modern stuff.' She laughed at my startled expression, and her guests, who had been drinking whatever she had given them, would call out: 'Grow up, boy, grow up!' I disappeared.

My father took refuge in his bedroom where he was trying to say his prayers, his hands covering his ears to block out the din which he must have found fairly painful. As for me, I would leave the flat, although once or twice, Ted, noticing my serious expression, would sidle up to me, take me by the arm, and would announce that he wanted to discuss philosophy with Julian. This was just what Julian did not want. Philosophy did not interest me. Only religion mattered, and I knew that Ted was a non-believer like all the rest. Furthermore, he had this way of making me feel ill at ease.

'You and I are going to sit down in a corner. You know, I love philosophy.'

'Yes, I know, but I have to go out.'

'Oh! So he's going to meet his girl friend. Tell me, what's she like? Brunette?'

I fled.

Typical Yankee, I thought. Ted came from New York. The others were nearly all from the North. Before the war, whenever a Northerner came to our home, we had to try to hide our feelings. Certain subjects had to be avoided; certain names, such as Sherman, were never mentioned, and we would never use the term 'Yankees' when referring to people from the North. Yet now, here were all these people from Massachusetts, Pennsylvania, New York State . . . My father's view was that, given the circumstances, it was best to let bygones be bygones, but what would my mother have said about that? All those nasal voices which droned on in our Southern ears . . . I think that once her initial anger had passed, she would have burst out laughing, perhaps crying a little as well, and she would have poured drinks for everyone.

I thought of her every day. Perhaps I was not as wicked as I imagined. I was certainly ridiculously vain, but there was something within me which I did not understand and which made up for my vanity. I have mentioned before that I could not bear to be touched. I did not like to be looked at either. Being looked at was like being touched by the eyes. I would hide as if I was ashamed, and if ever I did have to display myself, posing for a photographer for example, I would put on a proud look and stare defiantly. What was I frightened of? Did I think I might be attacked. I don't mean attacked physically, which was something I knew nothing about, but an attack on my secret and sacred inner self. My mother's remark about the body being the temple of the

Holy Spirit had marked me forever.

Because of all this, I was deeply troubled by Ted's presence. It brought back my childhood and the painting, *Les Porteurs de Mauvaises Nouvelles* ('The Bearers of Bad News'), the sight of which used to make my insides tighten up. He never realized this and neither did I. He was just a charming young sailor driven crazy by the pleasures of the flesh. As for me, I was a sort of living enigma who suffered because no one could guess what his problem might be, yet who had no idea himself what that might be. 'What's the point of being handsome?' I would ask myself, 'if no one is in love with me?' But I had built a wall of granite around me through talking about my religious vocation. *I was respected.* Ted was about the only one not to believe in all this nonsense, yet he frightened me.

At the beginning of July, I had a visit from James, the Jane Austen admirer. He was splendidly attired in a tailor-made sky-blue uniform of fine cloth, and boots which shone like mahogany.

Our conversation took place in the small sitting room, and I'm not sure why, but we stood by a rosewood bookcase. I gathered that in spite of his foreign nationality he had joined up as an apprentice in the French artillery school at Fontainebleau. One could get round the law by first signing on with the Foreign Legion, leaving immediately and then transferring to the French Army. It was all wonderfully simple and, at the end of five or six months, one left the school with a gold stripe.

As he spoke, James tapped his highly-polished boots with a leather switchstick and I could see the windows reflected from top to bottom in his toe-caps. I could see the attraction. All of a sudden, I mentally cast off my novice's cowl and saw myself dressed from head to foot in a sky-blue uniform, with boots.

This conversation with James has remained in my memory precisely because it was to be our last, although we never dreamt of suspecting so at the time. I remember that he spoke about Jane Austen again and also, poor fellow, about the friend with whom he was still in love. I chose the moment to say some pretty harsh things as kindly as I could, trying to make him see that the person in question was not worthy of his interest:

'He's a schoolboy', I told him, 'who just happens to be the top in his form.'

'Oh! You're right', he moaned, as if I had just brought him down to earth, and for a moment or two I believe he looked happy.

I explained to him just how odd it was to suffer as he did *for a boy*. 'At least if it had been a girl . . . ', I said with the cruelty of innocence.

He shook his head and did not speak. A few months later, in January 1919, he was struck by a bullet in the Boulevard Malesherbes, in the heart of Paris, fired by a policeman chasing a criminal. The stray shot killed James instantly. I think he must have been twenty. To have escaped death on the Argonne front only to end up on the pavement outside Félix Potin's grocery shop . . .

It was in July that I decided I would join the French Army as an infantryman rather than in the artillery. My father was in two minds. My sister Eléonore had immediately written from Genoa to say that the plan was tantamount to suicide, and my father tended to her opinion, but he had no objection to my joining the Americans at Fontainebleau. There were a few formalities that I've forgotten, then on 10

August of that year I reported to the town hall of the sixth *arrondissement*, where I had been summoned. In a room on the first floor, overlooking the church of Saint Sulpice, I met a captain and, seated behind him, an N.C.O. who was filling in papers. The captain asked me to undress, which rather shocked me. Was this why they had asked me to come here? I remembered everything I had been told about the black slave markets in the old South and I blushed violently. Take off one's clothes like a slave . . . Yet that is what I did. 'Take a few steps', commanded the officer. Burning inwardly, I took a few paces. 'This one's superb', he said as if he were talking about an animal. Clenching my teeth, I dressed again and signed some document. As an American, I was accepted into the Foreign Legion for twenty-four hours. It was possibly the most unexpected thing ever to have happened to me.

So it was that at Fontainebleau, in the early days of September 1918, I was once again part of a group of American boys who had joined up like me. We were given our own sky-blue uniform and in the little steel mirror, the instrument and accomplice of my continuing vanity, I looked to see whether I cut a fine figure. I should say that we all did much the same, for I think that most boys are narcissists. This did not include a boy called Gerald, who gave me a furtive look in the mirror, and who was indescribably ugly. One could only compare him to a moustachioed gargoyle. Anyway, we all spoke English, we were all dressed like French soldiers and we all slept in a long barrack room heated by a very basic stove. I learnt to make my bed in the regulation method and I did so very carefully for I was determined to obey every instruction. I liked everyone else, even Gerald who, I have to admit, was the sort who might have repelled me. My neighbour in the bed on the right in the barrack room was called Harold, and I'm not sure why, but I immediately felt an affection for him which even today I am unable to explain, but the feeling was reciprocated extraordinarily spontaneously. He was a bit taller and much stronger than I was, always sensible, and a model of perfection in my eyes, who never said or did anything unpleasant.

Among my other colleagues, I remember a boy of French extraction by the name of Remy. He had a small black moustache and laughed sarcastically at everything. If I remember correctly, he was a painter, but he also loved poetry. I can't recall who were his favourites, but he quoted one of the modern poets. 'He has written a remarkable poem', he said to me in his irritating voice. 'I'll recite the beginning: "Shit, here are some verses! . . . ".'. It's wonderful'. I burst out laughing and the line has stuck permanently in my memory.

There was also a French Jew called Klein. Klein was frightened, and, consequently, always wore a defiant expression. On his forehead there was a vein in the form of the letter Y. 'Youpin', he said. 'That's what they call us in French. So I have a Y on my forehead.' This remark made my heart bleed, for it was accompanied by a look that bore a combination of sadness, fury and despair. Everyone knew Klein was frightened. The war, humanity, the world itself, terrified him and yet, I don't know why, he always had a stubborn look about him, like that of some wretched animal that has been put in a corner. As a result, he inspired respect in me and I don't believe anyone ever dreamed of reproaching him on account of his race.

On the second day, we were sent to riding school and my first sight of these magnificent creatures somewhat alarmed me. They took me back to the strange dreams of my childhood, in fact, and evoked a world of confused and violent desires. I soon learnt to ride and I acquired a reasonably good seat, although I was always amazed when the horse lowered its neck to the ground, for from the rider's point of view it no longer appeared to have a head. Our instructor was a fierce young lieutenant who used to make us laugh because whenever he wanted us to trot rather than walk (which we preferred, for it was safer), he would shout out in his peculiar English: 'I *will* you trot!' In the end, the horses would quicken their pace, the noise grew louder and the walls of the riding school resounded to the sound.

The following week, we were taken on into the forest with our horses. Among us there was a tall, thin, bespectacled boy called Baker, already a good rider, who would give us all rather irritating advice. One day, he galloped up to me and shouted: 'You're upsetting your horse!' I gave him a look that could kill, but there was truth in what he said, for I pulled too hard on the bit and eventually my horse would take the bit with his teeth. He carried me at great speed. I could hear the massed beat of hoofs on the road and, dropping back a little, I allowed him to take me where he willed. Perhaps he was acknowledging that I had been innocent of the shameful error, but how natural it was to wrap my arms round his neck. A minute later, we had left the road and were crossing the forest at a fine gallop. A low branch could have broken my skull, but I never thought of danger, On the contrary, it was a voluptuous sensation to feel the nakedness of this magnificent creature between my legs. One of my childhood dreams was being accomplished. I was a centaur. I loved this horse and he knew it, for a horse's intuition is immediate and infallible, and it always knows what kind of person he is carrying. The pleasure I experienced was not erotic in the usual sense of that word, but I was still ecstatic with joy. It was as if I was flying, and at the same time was one with this majestic and powerful creature whose hoofs flew over the ground. After a while, he slowed his pace and, with a triumphant air, reluctantly took the path to the stables. That evening, I felt as if I had been beaten from top to toe, but I treasured the memory of this mad gallop through the still and watchful forest.

I will pass over the ballistic lessons, which bored me to death, and the rifle range exercises — the 75mm, the long 155mm — because these futile details are not worth remembering. On certain days, after four o'clock in the afternoon, we were free, and I used to go and sit on a bench in the park and read my Baudelaire, which I always carried in my pocket. I was on my own, and I would become intoxicated by this poetry and this prose in which I thought I heard a voice, a real voice. Whereas most books do not speak to one, this powerful voice would teach me anything I did not know; it taught me about the sadness of pleasure, the nothingness of the world and the attraction of this void, and my heart and mind would respond in a way they never did to any religious book, for in revealing the flesh in all its glory, it also produced an unfathomable melancholy. Again and again, I would be seduced and disillusioned. I could feel that the terror and the unconquerable fascination of sin affected him as it did me, but in launching himself into evil, the evil remained evil, and in some part of his mysterious heart, paradise shone out. I was not intelligent enough to appreciate the force of his inner contradictions, but I took them all in and I listened in wonder to this poet who spoke to me as no other poet has ever done in any language.

I had a kind of veneration for Baudelaire which I have retained all my life. I have read him wherever I went in the world and I would read him in a monastery if I were fortunate enough to be there on retreat. Nothing in him contradicts faith, and I would even say that his work is nourished by the very source that flows out of an Eden devastated by original sin. He is more of a Christian than many of those preachers who put one off religion by making it boring, and his stern gaze remains with us. I thought of all these things while watching the golden September sunset from the terraces at Fontainebleau.

In the town's bookshops I bought any book I could find by Léon Bloy. The best one can say about him is that he never makes religion seem dull and that was the tonic I needed, but what I did not realize was that there was a fanaticism that slumbered deep within me and it was reading Léon Bloy that aroused it. I required the absolute without having taken the intermediary path; I wanted many things to which I had no right, because I had never really led the simple Christian life, which is a life of love. I longed for the fruits of victory without ever having fought the battle. I resisted temptations only because those temptations were slight, not because I was strong. I did not know what it was to be tempted to the roots of one's courage; I knew nothing, yet in my pride I wanted to be a saint.

Having vowed never to kill anybody, one might ask why I joined the artillery. I can't answer that question. Perhaps, like many others I knew, I felt that the war was coming to an end, which considerably lessens any merit to be gained from offering my services.

Every Saturday, we were given twenty-four hours leave and, naturally, I would spend it in Paris (so did my colleagues, but for rather different reasons). The lieutenant who instructed us, a likeable fellow from Toulouse, spoke to me in confidence one day: 'Once a week, at your age, is quite enough.' I didn't know what he meant, or rather I didn't want to know, because in my chaste state of mind at the time, it shocked me. On Sunday mornings, I would go to High Mass at the chapel on the Avenue Malakoff, a vast building that belonged to the church of Saint Honoré d'Eylau. I listened wholeheartedly to the singing of the liturgy, I breathed in the incense and watched the lights shine on the high altar. Everything delighted me, even the rather unimaginative sermons given by Canon Soulange-Bodin. I was proud to be a Catholic. I believed my conscience was quite clear. Since God, according to me, had forgotten my sins, I could quite reasonably now count myself among the elect who, as we know, are small in number. In the afternoons, I would revel in the community singing in the chapel on the Rue Cortambert. These voices wafted over me like a wave and as I drifted, I knew complete happiness, the happiness of a child, of course, but then God treated me like a child. Has he ever treated me otherwise? It seemed to me that he had asked me to put my hand in his. There are some good souls whom he allows to walk ahead of him on the road. Not mine. It was too insecure, and it needed support, the support of a mother, for God is also a mother according to the prophet Isaiah. I needed to be able to feel, to see, to breathe. That was what my religion was like.

At military school, I was pretty hopeless at ballistics. We were given problems to solve which horrified me, for they brought back the childhood nightmares of figures, geometric shapes and strange terms, only one of which I recall because of the way our lieutenant from Toulouse pronounced it. He was a very gallant man with short legs, a black moustache and a marvellous accent. He reckoned I was a hopeless case, but he sensed that none of it was of much importance and that it was unlikely I would ever have to fire a shot. One day, in order to find out exactly how much we knew in French, he made us write an account of what we had seen at the front and what had particularly struck us. I chose to speak about the German prisoner of war camp I had seen in the Argonne. 'That is what made the greatest impression on me', I wrote, 'and it's quite enough to be going on with'. Why did I write this impertinent sentence? I cannot say, but it is the only one that I remember specifically. There was an element of pride deep within me that inspired these strange attitudes. I was irrationally stubborn. In any case, I do remember what it was I wrote about German prisoners. Having explained that ever since the war began, I, like everyone else, had been told that German soldiers were monsters, that they cut off the hands of children etc., I was surprised to see that those in the prisoner of war camp were no different to the rest of us. Some may say that I had the wrong attitude, but I am more proud of writing those lines, which have disappeared long ago, than many which I have published since. Today, I can scarcely remember those prisoners. With their hands in their pockets, standing with their legs wide apart, and their sullen expressions, there was something almost disdainful about the way they looked back at me, for they could only have seen a well-fed little American who had never fought in battle, and this kid in a uniform was inspecting them as if they were animals in a zoo. The glance one of them gave me has snagged in my memory. On this occasion, the arrogance was on the other side of the barbed wire.

One day, when I was taking off my kit in the barrack-room, I saw Klein come in, but it was a Klein I did not recognize. Throwing his beret and his riding crop on the bed, he looked calmly round the room and made some joke which I have forgotten. I soon learnt that he had worked minor miracles with the horse that had so terrified him, had made it perform some of the very hardest turns and manoeuvres, and had drawn gasps of admiration from the onlookers. Unfortunately, I had not seen any of this fine display as I was probably far away on my own horse who always took me to exactly wherever he wished to go, but I soon heard the flattering rumours which redeemed Klein in everyone's eyes. From now on Klein no longer bothered about the Y-shaped vein that pulsated on his forehead. Quite simply, he had become a different person. This transformation always struck me as a sort of inner miracle.

The eleventh of November 1918 fell on a weekday, much to the irritation of the students at the school, for they knew there would be huge, wild, patriotic parties going on all over the capital. How daft it was to celebrate armistice in such a sleepy small town! There were some rather pathetic Chinese lanterns that lit up the sad façade of the town hall and on a damp evening some fifty or sixty people gathered to watch the depressing spectacle. After a few fireworks, they all went home to bed. I walked along the main street, trying to raise my spirits and not succeeding, because we had already been expecting this virtually certain news for several days. I was happy, but just as I still do today, I needed a little time for the mood to register. In the same way, bad news does not affect me straight away. In my case, emotion always affects me after the event, which explains the inexplicably calm way I react to both good and bad tidings. With my hands in my greatcoat pocket, I wandered this way and that. For about the twentieth time,

I read the mysterious notice that was nailed to a wooden board under the entrance to the huge gates of the town prison. Private So-and-So had been condemned to several days of solitary confinement for having tried to harm a local girl. There was nothing difficult to understand about that.

But just below it, there was another notice giving advice to young soldiers about relationships with women and how to avoid serious diseases. I remembered my Uncle Willie, and the mere fact of reading these stark sentences terrified me and made me feel as if I was already contaminated, though I nevertheless stayed long enough to read the last few words which intrigued me beyond measure: 'Be selfish. Take your pleasure and go!' What could that possibly mean? As I returned to the school, I congratulated myself on the fact that I had no wish to harm anyone and expose myself to the nightmare of syphilis. What a disturbing world we lived in! Why did there have to be this strange act which perverted everything, these mad desires, this infernal disease which tracked lovers down? I longed for a different world in which mankind would perpetuate itself in some other way, without passion or brutality. There would be no more suffering. A child's heart would beat in every breast. In my naïveté, I did not realize that a vision like that was worthy of a lunatic asylum. Our earth was already a vale of tears. All the victories of childhood could make it no more nor less than a hell. But I had not yet read Freud.

I don't know what happened next. Between 11 November 1918 and the beginning of 1919, there is a blank. All I know is that at about that time, certainly before Christmas of 1918, we left the school with a magnificent gold stripe on our sleeves, a stripe in the shape of a V which was positioned half way up the forearm. All of us passed the exam, even me with my rather cheeky drawings in which I suggested that the local church, school and the town hall should be shooting targets, but they ignored this nonsense. The war was over. We were given our V-shaped stripes as a present and told that, depending on our wishes, we could either be demobbed forthwith, or we could spend a few weeks — as long as we wanted — in occupied territory.

I returned home on 3 January and told my father that I wanted to become a monk on the Isle of Wight. Can I ever forget the scene? My sister Anne was there. We were all standing in the dining-room and Anne had her arm round my neck and was crying. 'Daddy, don't let him go!' she said. My father thought for a moment and then said: 'Since they're offering to send you to Germany, I think you should accept. You may never have the opportunity again to see that country. While you're there, you must think hard about what you want to do, and when you come back, you will tell me what you have decided. You can then do whatever you wish.' I knew it was impossible to disobey my father. I had never said no to him or to my mother in my life. So I agreed, and the next day I left, not for the Rhineland, but for Brittany where the regiment to which I had been assigned was stationed, and whose barracks were then at Rennes.

Under a rain-drenched sky, this city struck me as a very sad place. I liked the old wooden buildings, and the house where du Guesclin* lived, but I was rather appalled by the cathedral which was neither Gothic nor Romanesque, but eighteenth-century. I was such an odd creature that the

* Bertrand du Guesclin (1320–1380), High Constable of France, a title abolished in the seventeenth century. (*Tr.*)

idea of praying in a church of that period made me feel guilty, but that's the way I was. At the barracks, I was put in a room normally reserved for an officer, although I took my meals in the NCO's mess. I only ate there once and I didn't touch a thing. I had scarcely sat down when I got up and left the room, for no sooner had soup been served in a huge pot placed in the middle of the table, than the sergeant, to hoots of laughter, drew out of the steaming liquid a large rat which had drowned in it. Without saying a word, I hoisted my leg over the bench on which we were seated and ran for the door. I was not seen in the mess again.

That evening I wandered through the street, and since I only had a few francs on me, I treated myself to some buckwheat biscuits which I bought from a bakery on a windy corner. The streets were poorly lit. There were hardly any passers-by and I strolled from one side of the street to the other not knowing what to do with my time. Suddenly, I heard someone whistling behind me and, turning round, I saw two American soldiers. They were so tall, rosy-cheeked and good looking that I was quite taken aback. They both wore perfectly cut uniforms, caps slightly tilted over their foreheads, light beige gaiters which looked almost white, and an armband with the initials M.P.(Military Police). As they walked past me, I heard one say to the other: 'He's an officer. Should we salute him?' His friend looked at me, must have reckoned I looked rather childish, and replied softly: 'No point'. It occurred to me to speak to them in English, but there was something so effortlessly superior about them that I held back. They strolled by like gods and one of them was softly singing a song about the pleasures of having a girl sitting on one's knees. This encounter upset me dreadfully and I never quite understood why it had such an effect on me. Even today, I can still hear the voice of the soldier singing, and it takes me back so far into the past that I feel almost dizzy.

I was in such a state of spiritual ardour that I found the cold nights and the empty spaces to my liking. A few days beforehand, I had written to Father Crété and he replied by return to say that as he was in Vannes and had to return to Paris, he would make a short stop at Rennes in order to see me. I can't really remember how all this was to be arranged. At Rennes, he would stay at the hospice of St Melaine and so it was agreed that I should meet him at the station, which I did. In that dark and sinister place, at seven o'clock in the evening, I found him wrapped in a large black cloak. He complimented me slightly ironically on my elegant uniform, then we took a hansom to St Melaine and went up to his room. Before he had even taken off his cloak, he said to me: 'My child, allow me to embrace you.' I was so unused to ecclesiastical customs that when I saw that he was bending towards me, I kissed him on each cheek, while he merely brushed my face with his. He then spoke to me about the great grace that had been shown to me, of his admiration for my father who was not at all opposed to my vocation ('He's a Christian, my child.'), and everything he said induced in me a feeling of inner excitement such as I had never known. I can still see the frozen room, the priest standing with a large suitcase at his feet, speaking to me in a pleading voice, and his piercing gaze which seemed to go right through me. So strong was my desire to be there that for a few moments I thought I was already in Paradise.

What happened the next day? I don't know. I believe Father Crété stayed a day or two longer in Rennes where he had things to do and I am almost sure that I attended a Mass he said where I was the only person present. I bought a cheap copy of Marguerite-Marie Alacoque's* autobiography and read it in a few hours. This strange book had what I would have called a magical effect on me were it not for the fact that it was about religion, for it took me out of this world and, even now, I am unable to read certain passages without the sense of being transported to some distant place. That awkward, noble and outdated language worked like a filter within me. For others the deathly delights of sin as described by Boccacio! I wanted to be saved, and somewhere deep within me, I could feel that surge of the Christian soul longing for release from his earthly body that St Paul speaks about.

I have a sense that at this point in my account something is missing, and that graces were being bestowed on me which I am unable to describe, both because I was not exactly conscious of them at the time and because my memory is weak. What is certain is that from September or October 1918 I experienced a religious zeal which continued to increase up until the end of that winter. I remember enjoying feeling hungry and cold in the streets of Rennes because it brought me closer to the Gospel. Marguerite-Marie's little verses, far from making me smile, induced in me an indescribable state. It was as if the houses all around me no longer existed, as if everything visible were fading and giving way to a happiness which knew no name.

> Love triumphs, love exults
> The love of the pure Heart rejoices!

I would repeat these words to myself in a sort of ineffable

* A French nun who lived 1647–90; she was canonized in 1920. (*Tr.*)

fear, for I knew the immediate effect they would have on me. My heart would start to thump as if it were responding to the beating of another heart and I had the impression that millions of voices were singing these verses from incalculable heights.

I no longer ate at the barracks, on account of the rat, and I believe I lived on pancakes, for I had very little money, but I did not stay long in Rennes and on the train that took me to Paris a few days later, I found myself sitting next to Father Crété. Why? Here my memory lets me down once again. I can still visualize the scene without being able to explain it. I can remember that the priest could only travel a little way with me. Was he going back to Vannes, or elsewhere? I really don't know, but I remember that the compartment was full and, with all those people watching, he asked me about my stay in Rome and that while I was naïvely extolling the virtues of St Peter's, he asked me whether the church was Gothic or Romanesque. Did he do this deliberately to make himself appear ignorant? I wonder. In any case, instead of evading the question as I should have done had I been rather more kind or subtle, I considered it with a slightly surprised look and replied pointedly: 'Neither the one nor the other, Father. It's Renaissance.' 'Ah?' he said modestly, and nodded like someone who has just been chastised in school. I immediately felt rather embarrassed, but how could I withdraw what I had said? A moment later, we parted.

Before continuing this account, I must say something about an apparently rather pointless visit I made to Brest. I cannot remember very much about the town apart from a narrow street at dusk with a fine rain falling. As I often did when I was discovering a town for the first time, I walked about saying over and over to myself the following words: 'You're in Brest, wandering around a place that you've never seen before.' I would have forgotten all of this were it not for one particular detail that comes back to me. I had been dining in a fairly modest restaurant and not far from my table was a group of people who were talking loudly and, among them, was a large man with a red face. I ate quickly and, as it happened, I left the restaurant at the same time as these people who had obviously eaten and drunk a great deal. As he walked past me, the large red-faced man gave me a knowing look and called out in a rough voice: 'Now let's buy ourselves a bit of love!' I was horrified by what he said because the words 'buy' and 'love' were so brutally conjoined. I remember that after we had parted, I found myself in a badly lit street and I was overcome with a feeling of extraordinary sadness. It was drizzling and the cobbles in the road shone like metal. That was all I saw.

I had hardly returned to Paris before I told my father once again of my decision to become a monk. Had I been given leave to spend a few days at home? I don't remember. I had orders to rejoin my regiment in Metz where it had now been posted. I can do no more than relate things as they come to mind. One morning, my father told me that since I had been baptized, I should now receive the sacrament of Confirmation, and so he was going to take me to the church of the Holy Ghost Fathers where the Archbishop of Paris was due to administer the sacrament to several people. Is it not odd that I am obliged to write that I had only the vaguest idea of what it was all about? Was some sort of preparation necessary? I didn't know. As usual, I did everything my father wished. I can see myself now, in a chapel, kneeling by a pillar, with eight or ten others. A nun hands me a folded piece of paper which I open and read the name Michael. 'This will be your Confirmation name', says the nun. I remain kneeling, my heart thumping, as Monsignor Amette approaches, bends over each one of us, and when he reaches me, gives me a light tap on the cheek while uttering some prayers before continuing on his way. I have forgotten everything else except that when I got home, I wrote a deliriously happy letter to the American nun* I have mentioned previously and who was then living in Angers. This letter, whose childish language has remained in my memory, much to my embarrassment, is the only proof I have that I received the sacrament of Confirmation under the required conditions and in spite of my ignorance, and came away to my astonishment with *Quis ut Deus* (Who is like God?), the prince of the heavenly host, as my patron saint.

I must have left for Metz on 20 or 22 January. It is a city to which I have never returned and I have only a hazy recollection of its dark, muddy streets and the gloomy, rather sinister mass of its cathedral. I was allowed an hour or two there , and so I think I must have completed my papers and received my travel permit at the barracks. In any case, I do remember that I was ordered to report at Haguenau where further instructions would be given me, and I also remember being questioned about that splendid, legendary character, the Gunner of Metz, who was a hero of mine since I was also a gunner, although I'd never been given any information about the celebrated soldier or taught the words of the song about him. Once or twice, I

* See *The Green Paradise*

had asked colleagues to fill in this gap in my knowledge, but they laughed, saying that my modesty would be shocked and I didn't dare insist. He probably behaved, I thought, like those characters in Mr Kreyer's horrible albums, and at the time I was bothered very little by any of that . . .

I felt calm and far removed from a world which I believed in less and less; that world in which one saluted officers and travelled by railway. This reminds me of something I should have mentioned earlier. One evening in October 1918, when I was at the cinema with one of my sisters, I saw on the newsreel a scene which had been filmed just behind the front line during one of the last battles of the war. An idea occurred to me which I wanted to jot down immediately and so I scribbled a few words on the first bit of paper I found in my inside coat pocket: my enlistment papers with the Legion. I wrote that what I was watching on the screen might not be true, that the war, the entire war, was no more than an illusion or, in other words, a projection of something within ourselves. Quite simply, the outside world did not really exist in the way we saw it. One could not even prove that it existed. All that really existed was within me, inside my own head; I was unable to see it, but as long as I was happy and at peace with myself, I was able to see trees, water and hills, though whenever I was upset, I would see men fighting, huge guns, and earth being thrown up by exploding shells. On this basis, in what sense could one's neighbour be said to exist? He existed in the way I did, susceptible to the same illusions, but he didn't see exactly what I saw because we were different, because I was unlike anyone else. Where he might see the colour blue, for example, I would see black, and it was just that we could not agree on what to call it. His blue corresponded to what I thought of as black. But according to this line of thinking, which I found fascinating, what became of the reality of my face? My answer was that my face corresponded to an idea that I had of myself. What was questionable was matter. Images were true, but they were only images. Reality lay behind all this, and essentially it was invisible. I don't know where these strange ideas came from but they certainly influenced me for years to come and I can see traces of them in all my work.

I had a sense of elation which I did not mention to anyone and, folding the sheet of paper which I tucked into my pocket, I felt a sudden liberation from the visible world and everything in it that was sad or mediocre. The great secret had been revealed to me. All the wonderful books that I had read, the paintings in the Louvre, the statues, all those things — they were me, they were in my imagination. Others might imagine different things, but everything I could actually see delighted me. In this way, Ted's face was an exceptionally beautiful thought, so was Roger's, my friend at the lycée, but what Roger did with others was the visible sign of an inner sin, a sign without any reality in itself. Everything was within one.

So what became of religion in all this? Religion was the only truth. Its words were true because they were effective. But the priest's vestments, the cross on the altar? They were signs of an invisible but undeniable truth. I went further. The consecrated host? The consecrated host was the one reality in a world of appearances. In the same way, when Christ came on earth, he really did exist in a nightmare world. His hand was a real hand, his eyes, real eyes.

I can't say that these ideas have ever really left me. There is still a smattering of them and they explain much of my behaviour in the world that we call reality, but there is so much one could say on this point and, anyway, is it really of any importance? If I mention it, it is because this account is not exactly what the Germans call a *Lebensbeschreibung*, but more of a journey, an inner exploration of myself. No doubt I do believe in the reality of words, of paper, of this hand which is writing, but not to excess.

With such a bizarre philosophy, did my neighbour not become a ghost? Well, no. On the contrary, I had an idea that I ought to save him, a notion which often made me say things I did not mean, as I shall reveal later. But where did my suspicions about the real existence of the world of the senses come from in the first place? I really do not know. I had never read much philosophy, but through God's grace and thanks to my mother, I had an unshakeable faith in the invisible. From this came the conclusion that the world we see is a reality that is shallower and even debatable, was a simple step for an imagination like mine. Some biblical phrases came to my aid: 'My kingdom is not of this world' (this world was therefore suspect). 'The prince of this world . . . the god of this world'. Prince and god of nothingness.

It is strange to think that it is usually carnal experience that is considered necessary to make a man of a boy. I lacked carnal knowledge. In this way a sort of intellectual childishness remained intact until my twenty-second year. A certain quality of faith was also preserved which was only threatened by emotional turmoil well after adolescence. Because of this, and despite all my efforts to persuade myself to the contrary, it never entirely disappeared from my heart. Later, I turned away from Christ, because he hampered the fulfillment of my carnal desire, but I did not dare to reject him totally. I tried to ignore his existence, but I would not have him forget mine.

I lived my life as if I had just woken from a dream, and it was in such a state that I travelled to Haguenau where I reported to an officer seated behind a table. Hearing that I was American, he asked me all the usual questions, and after a few banal but good-natured remarks, he handed me a piece of paper which told me to wait at a certain street corner for a car which would take me to my destination.

At this point there occurs one of the most lucid memories of my entire life. I was standing on the corner of a street at dusk when I saw a small horse-drawn, canvas-covered wagon approaching. It stopped in front of me and a young soldier jumped down, saluted me and addressed me as '*mon lieutenant*', which rather tickled me since I was not sure whether I was an officer or not, and we both drove off to the station to collect my trunk. The soldier took charge of everything. I remember that it was a freezing evening and he insisted on covering my knees with a rug, for a gale was blowing through the wagon which was poorly protected by the canvas covers.

I no longer remember the name of the village where we were bound, but we were over two hours on the road and, above the vast stretch of the snowline, I could see the moon and stars shining out of the black sky. My companion did not speak much and it was so cold that I think he dozed off from time to time, while I, for my part, was overcome my a sense of happiness that was so strange and overwhelming that I have never experienced anything like it since. The snow muffled the noise of the wheels and the horses' hoofs, and the cold air bit my ears, but I had the feeling of being detached from myself and it was as if I was entering some strange and splendid kingdom. The word firmament kept coming to mind because it was a word that seemed to sparkle and which reached me from the depths of an abyss in a voice that was both loud yet silent. What did it say? I would not have had the slightest idea. The voice spoke, however; it spoke to me, and when it did, I felt happy. If only I could have understood what it said. Many years were to pass before I heard the voice again and that night, on a road in Alsace, without realizing it, I said goodbye to an entire part of myself.

It must have been about nine o'clock at night when we arrived at the village whose name I have forgotten, but which must have been on the road to Wissembourg. It was a typical Alsatian village: there were houses with huge tilting roofs like castles depicted on postcards, although I could not see much apart from the snow on the ground and these enormous vertical roofs against a backdrop of an amazing night sky sprinkled with stars. I had the feeling I was walking inside a Christmas card and my mood of gaiety was only tempered by the prospect of shortly having to introduce myself to strangers. It was very dark despite the glow that came from the white landscape. The soldier took my trunk and showed me towards a door which he opened. We found ourselves in a badly lit corridor and when we came to another door, the soldier told me to knock, and then he left me.

Being shy, I knocked gently. A few seconds later, I was astonished to find myself in a small, over-heated room where three officers were seated around a table. The mere act of writing these words on the page makes me feel that I am back within those walls, waiting for something to happen. Why don't these men say anything? I salute rather awkwardly without introducing myself, and since they have taken their berets off, I remove mine. They look amazed. Were they not expecting me? Suddenly, the oldest of them, a lieutenant, stands up; the others do the same and walk towards me, laughing.

'Are you the officer cadet they were sending us?' asks the lieutenant.

He mentions his name and I give him mine.

'We were laughing,' he explains, 'because you are not at all as we imagined. We'd been told it was to be an American. We thought you would be wearing glasses and that you would not know a word of French.'

All three looked so relieved that I began to laugh too. The lieutenant was a heavily built young man whose very black hair framed his pale, energetic face. The sub-lieutenant looked like a wild animal, probably because of his receding profile and his reddish hair. These two men greeted me very warmly in loud voices, which made me feel ill at ease because I could not speak to them in the same way, and their familiarity unsettled me.

The third officer stood slightly apart and was the last to shake my hand, muttering his name, which I was unable to catch, as he did so. It is with some emotion that I speak of him, for I have never forgotten him and he once uttered a phrase which has remained in my heart and has never left. I wonder if he is still alive and whether he remembers me.

He was about my height, perhaps a shade taller and more slender, and he had a certain elegance. This was what one first noticed about him. With his reserve and a sort of natural dignity, he had the grace of a dancer, and in fact he walked like a dancer, with a light, elastic step which made one think he was walking on the tips of his toes. His very bright eyes, set in a thin face with fine features, watched me carefully, but he turned away the moment he was introduced. I sensed an extreme politeness about him and felt that his colleagues' behaviour slightly irritated him.

This first impression was so strong that it eclipsed any others and I have no memory of how the evening ended, nor where we slept, or what we did the next day. I only remember that a few days later we left this village to go on to another.

The four of us rode on horseback in step, followed by the soldiers with their guns. It all sounds so unlikely that it seems strange that this should ever have been part of my life. However, one night we arrived in a village in Alsace where we were billeted on local families. I was alone in my room and I remember that on waking the next morning I ran to the window to see where we were. I saw a large farmyard, clean and well maintained, and although there was nothing extraordinary in that, I was nevertheless amazed, for it all seemed so familiar to me that I wondered where I had seen it before. That was clearly impossible because I had never been to Alsace before, yet later, walking around the village, I had the same sensation so clearly on several occasions that it was like the key to a mystery which I was always on the point of unlocking but never quite succeeding. Nevertheless, I experienced to the root of my being a sense of total happiness that was both reassuring and inexplicable. How beautiful those huge wooden houses looked under the snow! I did not dare tell my companions that it seemed to me that I had known them all my life. Besides, they would have taken me for an eccentric even sooner than they did.

The day after next, the lieutenant told us that we were going to cross the frontier into Germany. I was very curious as to how we would be received. The four of us made our way to the border, and we kept silence as we took our first few steps on German soil, walking through a village whose pretty houses were painted in ochre and sea-green. The inhabitants stood by their doors and the children were huddled against their mothers. Not a word was spoken, and the only sound was that of our horses' hoofs and the noise of the cart-wheels on the cobbles. I tried to read something from the faces of those who watched us but one might as well have looked for an expression on a stone wall.

We all wore our sky-blue greatcoats and our berets and I was careful to sit well on my horse and to look as casual as the others appeared to be, but I was really choked with emotion. It was no small matter to cross into Germany, on horseback and in uniform, after a long war, even if one hadn't been involved in the fighting. I looked around me determined not to forget anything.

Was it that same evening or the evening of the next day? We arrived in a delightful little town overlooking a deep valley which reminded me of an Old Testament illustration. I can see myself in a humble peasant's room with two beds side by side where all four of us were gathered at the end of a cold, bright day. Through the two small windows we could see the long valley under a red sky and between the windows there hung a heavy mirror with black frames. I looked at myself in this mirror.

This particular moment is so ingrained in my memory that I cannot help dwelling on it a little. I only understood its full significance much later. There were two reasons for the pleasure I took in observing myself in the mirror, the first being that I was wearing my black uniform for the first time, the second, stranger one, was that my colleagues, far from teasing me as they should have done, kept quiet and watched me carefully. I remember that as I walked into this room, the youngest of these officers, a cadet like me, was on his own. I was worried that he might laugh at me but, as far as I recall, he did not say a word. At that moment, the lieutenant and the sub-lieutenant, who had been in the

dining-room next door, walked into the room. The lieutenant made some jovial remark which I have forgotten, but it
will be a long time before I forget what the sub-lieutenant
said. He smiled and circled around me with his head bent
forward like a fox, then he congratulated me, and it was at
that moment I caught sight of myself in the mirror. I saw
not only my own reflection (I wonder what became of
religion and the Isle of Wight in this account) but also three
serious and watchful faces. Eventually the sub-lieutenant
broke the silence: 'There are two beds in this room. The
instructions are that the two youngest should sleep in the
same room. Is that O.K. with you, cadet?' The question
was not addressed to me, but to my colleague who held the
same rank. 'Just as he wishes', he replied.

I said I would prefer to sleep on my own. The cadet
turned away sharply and I was given another room where,
in fact, I slept alone. What gaffe had I committed? Did they
think me impolite? When the four of us dined together that
evening, I noticed that they were less friendly to me. I
admit I was chattering somewhat thoughtlessly, because I
felt happy, but gradually I stopped speaking and I believe
we finished dinner in total silence. I say 'I believe', for I am
not sure, but what I do remember is that just before we
retired to go to bed, the sub-lieutenant came up to me, and
on the pretext of saying something flattering, he swore at
me in an incredibly coarse way.

I don't know what would have happened if I had
understood what he said, but the words he used remained
meaningless to me. Perhaps this is why I remember them so
precisely, for it was about four years before I came to know
what they meant. I glanced at him and laughed. 'What
does that mean?' I asked. I caught an expression of anger
and supplication in the eyes of the cadet as he looked at the
sub-lieutenant, who left without saying good-night. The

cadet, on the other hand, did bid me good-night in his firm and gentle voice, and with that look that hovered between a forgot-me-not and a slab of steel. How different he was to the others! Yet this entire scene which remained so clear and yet mysterious in my mind meant nothing to me. I did not ask myself any questions and I don't know who slept in the room with two beds. Alone in my bedroom, I carefully took off the black uniform in which I thought I had dazzled everyone and, having said my prayers, I went to bed and fell asleep.

Needless to say, I would not have been able to afford this uniform had it been made by a tailor, but it was simply my American ambulance driver's uniform which I had had dyed black, with a triple red band added to the trousers and my splendid gold stripes with red braid which I had sewn onto the sleeves.

Having left the small town, we rode in the direction of the Saarland. I had come to know my companions better, thanks to the long conversations we had on the road and at meal times. The lieutenant and sub-lieutenant had had a tough time of it at the front. One day they took me aside and told me that the cadet, who was a year older than me, had seen action and fought very well in 1918, and that his bravery had made a strong impression. I was not surprised. I could see that from his eyes, even though he looked like a girl and would cry when provoked. I guessed that the two men were very fond of him, but their confiding in me seemed misplaced. As far as I was concerned, my feelings for this boy did not go beyond the sympathy I felt for all my companions. He did not particularly interest me, not to begin with at least, and I did not have much to say to him. Once, one of the two officers made some remark about his good looks, and I saw him blush and look away very gracefully. Handsome, the cadet? I wondered what they could mean. Of course, he was blond and the gods were blond. Certainly, his eyes were beautiful, as were his small, narrow nose, his mouth and his ears. He was a very handsome young man, but he lacked a certain fire and strength. He made up for that with a wonderful expression which he wore to create whatever distance he judged necessary between him and whoever was speaking to him. He did not need to show me the crest on his signet ring to let me know that he came from a good family. I was touched by this rather naïve gesture. I let him explain the crest and duly admired it.

As chance would have it, a few days later he and I were lodged in the same house and the same room. I have forgotten the name of the German village, but I remember the room perfectly. It was long, with two large windows that had no curtains or shutters, and it gave onto the street. The beds were not side by side; instead, one was an extension of the other, and I chose the one nearest the window. The idea of spending the night in the same room as someone else did not exactly please me, but this time I had not been consulted. The lieutenant had given orders which I obeyed.

It was bitterly cold, and I undressed as quickly as possible without looking at my companion, but, quick as I was, he was in his bed before me and I could see his good-looking face on the pillow watching me. I was under my covers in a flash and we began to chat. I don't know what we found to say to each other, but suddenly he pointed out that we had not turned out the light and that the switch was by the door.

'Do me a favour, will you?' he asked. 'Could you switch off the light? I'm so snug in my bed.'

'Oh, I'm frozen to death in mine.'

'Well, that's why . . . '

What could he mean? I laughed, jumped out of bed and ran to the door to switch off the light. It was then that something very strange, certainly the strangest moment of my youth, occurred. Having turned off the light, I stood, barefoot and motionless in the darkness, and I suddenly felt tempted to jump into the cadet's bed. I had no idea where this urge came from and, no doubt, that was why I did not give way to it. There was a deep silence and with a sense of wonder I remember noticing that the outlines of the windows were reflected on the floor by the silvery light of the full moon. How clearly I can visualise the scene again in my memory today! I jumped into bed, without hesitating this time, and bid my companion good-night, although I don't remember whether he replied. Under my blankets, I congratulated myself for not having done anything so ridiculous. Was I really mad? What would this Frenchman have thought of me if I had approached him and slipped into bed beside him? Without any doubt, he would have beaten me up and made a good deal of fun of me. I could not understand where such a peculiar idea should have come from. Much later, I came to suspect that it did not come from within me but had been suggested to me.

What next? There is a series of blanks. What is certain is that by the end of January we had reached our destination which was a small town in the Saar called Oberlinxweiler. Here, my memories are fairly clear though interspersed with gaps. The house in which I was billeted was the last along the road out of the town and beyond it there was open countryside. My room was a large one, decorated with red tiles, and permanently icy. This constant cold, to which I paid little attention for I was only there to sleep, somehow represented the attitude of the house's inhabitants to my mind. In fact, I never actually saw any of them. Occasionally, I would hear someone whispering behind a door, but that was all. I undressed. I went to bed. In the morning, Jarras, my orderly, brought me some hot water and, a quarter of an hour later, I was out of the inhospitable place, taking my breakfast a hundred metres away in a house that was less forbidding and less clean, but resonant with loud voices, for the lieutenant and the sub-lieutenant both spoke as if they were outside in the open air.

I feel as if I could paint the small dining-room with its canary-yellow walls where we gathered and spent long hours when the weather was bad. There was a big, square table, and above Leonardo's 'Last Supper' which hung on the wall, could be read these words: *Amen, amen dico vobis quia unus ex vobis traditurus est me.* A terrifying sentence which I must have read and re-read at least a hundred times.

In the afternoons, alone with the cadet in the dining-room, I would open my Crampon Bible on the table and read the prophets and the gospel. It was a way of saying: 'For goodness' sake, leave me to my sublime aspirations and realize that I am not like you'. Yet, what else could I do, since all I wanted was to read the Bible and my own room was unheated? I nevertheless excelled at provoking discreet questions which I answered even more discreetly and with a mysterious smile, play actor that I was, and scarcely ten days had passed before it became generally known that I wanted to become a monk. How fascinating I suddenly became! I invented an invisible, portable cell for myself, a type that was easy to use, which allowed me to provide these men with an exhibition of a perfect soul on its way to heaven. Perhaps I am being a little hard on myself, but it was rather like that. Certainly, I believed with all my heart, but where, dear officer-cadet, where were the good works, the piety, the rosary, above all, the Mass? There were none of these, or if there were, they have completely escaped my memory. Yet I was in a Catholic country. Did it not occur to me to go to church? Apparently not. I read the Bible and said my prayers. These were the limits of my religion.

I wonder what my companions thought of me. Had I been a little more sensitive, I would have understood that in spite of the fact that they never said anything, they must have found me rather shallow, as became clear to me a little later on. At first they kept their remarks to themselves, because of what they had discovered about me, but they gradually started to talk about me with all the usual coarseness associated with a uniform. The only one who behaved with moderation was the fair-haired cadet who, glancing at me as if to excuse himself, gave me a knowing smile. As for me, I didn't say a word, I heard nothing, I locked the door of my invisible cell, I was entirely admirable, oblivious to everything.

I was oblivious to everything, yet I did not go to Mass. Why? I wish to know. Perhaps there was a reason. I loved the Mass and I loved the Church. So? Were there no priests in that region? It is possible. Yet I remember that one day the cadet and I went to see our chaplain (he must surely have said Mass . . .) and I still remember the charming and courteous way my companion spoke to him. Afterwards, I met this priest in the street on several occasions. He was a small, humble and rather shy man who seemed to enjoy conversing with me. Without any modesty, I showed off my small biblical knowledge. Perhaps I confided in him, and I am not sure I've got this right, but it seems to me now, for reason which I forget, I spoke to my colleagues in uniform about subjects that I withheld from the chaplain.

One day he offered me a poisoned pill in the form of a compliment, which I have retained, even if I have forgotten everything else he ever said to me: 'You are certainly the most interesting person I have met here.' 'Oh, Father!' Bow our heads and blush a little if possible, but what's that you were saying, Father? That I was the most interesting . . . ? Could you not develop this a little further? No? Nothing else? You have nothing to add? What a pity. But perhaps you knew something that I could not see myself: beyond my ridiculous behaviour at the age of eighteen, you saw God's infinite mercy.

In the cadet's eyes, I remained someone who was fairly inscrutable, and this fact in itself aroused a desire within me that I had never imagined before. I was so far from even suspecting what it was that I regarded him as a virgin, someone completely untrammelled. Perhaps he was in some ways. I doubt that he was a virgin like me, but his soul remained transparent. Life had not worn it down. Because of this, I saw the young lieutenant as a brave knight in shining armour, with his deep blue eyes hidden by a silver visor. To my mind, the sky-blue of his uniform was his colour, the one that best expressed his personality. That was how I wanted to see him in any case. The more I saw of him, the more I admired him. I knew that the Croix de Guerre that hung from his chest had not been won easily. For all sorts of confused reasons, I would sometimes feel drawn to him by a surge of affection, which was quickly crushed by one look from his blue eyes. If, in my simplicity, I behaved mysteriously, and there is no one whose reactions are as incomprehensible as those of a pubescent boy, he was even more mysterious, but I used to like to observe him in a rather absent-minded way. I liked him very much without being especially interested in him. He could keep his secrets for all I cared. I gave up bothering about what it was he wanted from me. I would meet his coldness with a constant good humour which used to irritate him. I would make fun of him and I would so annoy him with my teasing that we gradually came to know each other better; his response would be a look of fury which improved his good looks still more, but failed to distance us as he might have hoped, for I regarded myself as his equal and would laugh to his face.

Had I been more intelligent and more human, I would have understood him and loved him, but I was disturbed by the things the lieutenant and sub-lieutenant said about him. They chatted quite openly about him, and sometimes even to his face, about his frustrated and tormented desires. He needed girls and for some reason he could not find any in the district. 'Impure,' I would say to myself, 'he's impure. Yet how can he be, when his colour is blue?'

I believe that the boy's reserved manner towards me was due to his own frustration. He never laughed or spoke much. No doubt my antipathy to matters of the flesh exasperated him. One day, when the four of us were strolling around the neighbourhood, the lieutenant pointed to a charming, somewhat isolated small house and said: 'There's a house that would suit the cadet. He could spend every day and night there for a month with a pretty German blonde.' 'Why a blonde?' asked the cadet with a melancholy smile. I listened in silence to their jokes. I couldn't help thinking there was something seductive about the notion, but a minute later, I had forgotten all about it.

On another occasion, it was decided we should go to Neunkirchen to see the blast furnaces. I had no desire to visit the blast furnaces, but I said yes, because I nearly always said yes when I though it might please someone. So we caught the train and there we were, the four of us, alone in a small compartment, laughing and joking even more than usual. Why all this jollity, I wondered vaguely. In any case, I was happy. There was a holiday atmosphere. The sun was shining on the fields which I thought looked lovely. 'Aren't they beautiful?' said one of the officers in a voice that was pleasant but which I thought was slightly strange. They spoke to me rather as one speaks to a child. Then, suddenly, something happened which seemed quite inexplicable to me, for in spite of my age I was scarcely more than a child. The cadet stood up, and while everyone else laughed, told me exactly what he thought of me. He used a short and brutal expression, a rough soldier's expression, which left me stunned. I smiled and told him to shut up. The officers laughed even more loudly. Too loudly, it seemed to me, and once again I had the sense that I was missing something, that for some reason I did not understand, I had upset them.

How could this boy who was normally so haughty have used such an expression? He must have been joking, I told myself; he wanted to shock me, to show that he was a soldier in front of the officers. The next day, he was polite but rather distant. I felt strongly that he did not care for me and would happily have insulted me.

I have forgotten to mention that on one of my walks I made the acquaintance of a young local primary school teacher, but I can't remember how this came about. Perhaps I had asked her the way. Of all the inhabitants of Niederlinxweiler, she was the only one who had more than ten words to say to me. For everyone else, I was some sort of ghost who was scarcely noticed, but Mlle Martha was much kinder and would invite me for coffee at her father's house.

He was never to be seen in the small living-room which was full of large armchairs and green plants, but as far as I know I was welcome there, because I was cheerful and certainly unaffected. Mlle Martha, who was plump and rosy, had prepared the coffee and cakes herself. We talked about Goethe and Schiller. I preferred Goethe because he had been handsome in his youth, but this seemed a frivolous point of view to Mlle Martha, who preferred Schiller's ardent spirit. Our little discussions took place at about four o'clock when she returned from school. With shining eyes, she would often tell me: 'Today I had to smack a child!'

'Really?'

'Yes.'

And with a laugh she waved her hand up and down. It was quite clear, even for a boy as uninformed as I was, that she took an obvious pleasure in correcting young people. We both laughed. Sometimes, she would go down into the cellar and would come back with a small pet goat called Ziegelchen, which she would stroke. I would kiss Ziegelchen on the top of his head and then she would lead him away. One day, my friend the cadet, who was game for any new experience, asked if I would take him with me to Mlle Martha's. With pleasure! We arrived and I introduced him, but there was a moment of awkwardness, for a friend of Mlle Martha's was there too, a rather well built lady who was getting on for fifty. She gave us a stern look, then she rose to her feet and, proffering each of us a stiff hand, said: 'If you were English I would not shake your hands, but as you're French, I will, in spite of everything.' Coffee and cakes appeared (I could not help laughing to myself when I thought of my English grandfather) and the lady leant over towards Mlle Martha: 'They're nice looking, both of them, but they are rather lacking in character.'

We showed her the palms of our hands and my friend's signet ring made an immediate impression on her. A title! A crest! She read the lines on Herr Graf's [the Count's] hands first and predicted a fine future for him. Herr Graf had remarkable qualities. She listed them. I watched with amazement as this woman grovelled in such a shameless way in front of a boy thirty years younger than her. She gave him a big smile, then looked absent mindedly at my hands, saw nothing exceptional, pressed the flesh around the base of my thumb and simply said: 'Mmm!' After which she got to her feet and took her leave.

My friend and I went home, and I assume he was disappointed, for he never suggested that we visit Mlle Martha's house again. I can't imagine what sort of dream woman he was expecting. In any case, I went back there the next day and asked her why her friend had murmured 'Mmm' as she squeezed the thickest part of my hand. 'Oh!' she said, 'one can't explain it. That's the lifeline.'

'The lifeline? Then why did she say "Mmm"?'

'But I can't tell you!' she laughed. I asked again. She shook her head. 'Is it embarrassing?' She laughed again and I thought: 'She must mean that I have been impure. It must show.'

As a matter of fact, I had not been impure for a long time, but I had this notion that previous acts of impurity would somehow be indelibly marked on my face, for I seemed to see a shadow at the corner of my eyes which worried me more than one would believe possible. Mlle Martha laughed at my impatience and went on preparing her cakes.

I don't know what the cadet can have thought of these visits. He must have realized that they were completely innocent, but he kept an eye on me for other reasons and said to me one day: 'You know, you shouldn't eat too much, because you'll get fat and that would be a pity.' These words spoken in a soft voice seemed strange to me. Why should it matter to him if I put on weight? His whole manner seemed strange: his sudden anger as much as his good humour, and this sudden tenderness which sometimes softened his severe, ever watchful gaze. One day when we were riding our horses along the road, he slowed his pace and came up to me.

'Why are you so proud?' he asked.

'I'm no more proud than you.'

He beat his leg with his whip and exclaimed: 'Oh! You'll be impossible later on.'

I asked why, but all he said was: 'All your fine talk.'

Today I wonder about all this fine talk I was accused of. There is no doubt that I was loquacious, but what did I talk about? It can only have been about religion and my friend could not stand the subject. I am surprised he never hit me, for my rather frenzied piety was mixed with a naïve pride. He sat very upright on his horse, his shoulders thrown back, and looked at me with a kind of despair. At moments like those he struck me as very handsome but, I would ask myself, what on earth could be the matter with him?

I don't know how it came about that we found ourselves one day at a convent run by nuns in black habits. What were we doing there? All I remember is walking up the staircase which was highly polished and smelt of wax, and reaching a landing where, above a doorway, the following words were written in large gothic lettering:

EIN TAG IN DEINEN VORHOFEN IST BESSER DENN SONST TAUSEND!

I took my friend by the arm and whispered: 'Do you understand? One day in the house of the Lord is better than a thousand elsewhere! Oh! it's true,so true'. He smiled at me with all the sweetness of an angel.

We must have got on reasonably well, for it seems to me that we were hardly ever apart. One day there was an opportunity for us to go to Sankt-Wendel to hear a concert in a small theatre. We were given seats in the first row, a few feet away from the stage which was hidden by a rough linen curtain. I had only ever listened to music at home before now and I was so happy to be here that I found it hard to keep still. I would have liked to squeeze my friend's hand, but I didn't dare. The curtain had still not risen . . . Suddenly, out of the stillness, the choir of pilgrims from *Tannhäuser* could be heard. Never having heard a single note of Wagner, I did not know the music, but it seemed to me that we were transported to a different world. There was no orchestra. There were only these voices, but they were so pure and so plentiful that I was transfixed. Gradually, the curtain rose to reveal about thirty boys between the ages of twelve and eighteen, singing with extraordinarily serious expressions. I don't know what we heard after that, but I do remember that on the way home I reprimanded my friend for not having appreciated it sufficiently. 'Not bad!' I yelled. 'What more do you want?'

There were times when I could see from his eyes that he had a strong desire to provoke me, because he thought I did not respect him enough and because I continued to keep my distance, but the pretext he had been looking for presented itself a few weeks later.

One day I told my orderly to saddle my horse. What I

wanted to do was pay a visit to Mlle Martha, but instead of the horse I usually rode being brought to me, I was astonished to see an immense beast appear, with mad eyes and restless hoofs. It was explained to me that the lieutenant had taken my horse and this was the only other one available. I should have suspected that they wanted to play a trick on me and put me to the test. In any case, I was hardly in the saddle before we shot off like an arrow from a bow. The more I tugged at the horse's bit, the faster he galloped. Hell for leather, he crossed the astonished village and in what seemed to me a few seconds his hoofs ate up the distance that separated us from Niederlinxweiler. I was so surprised that at first I had no time to be frightened and just allowed myself to be carried along, but my anxiety turned to terror when we reached the road that crossed the approach to Niederlinxweiler, for I knew that this road led to another long road that descended so steeply it was almost vertical, and what would I do then? It so happened that having cleared the town's suburbs at a triple gallop, this horse, which I believed had come straight from Hell, stopped dead when he saw what must have appeared to be an abyss in front of him. I shall never know what got into his head, but the fact is he turned around and trotted back through the suburbs which, thank heavens, were virtually empty. At that moment I spotted Jarras, my orderly, and called out to ask him to take my horse back to Oberlinxweiler.

I was a few yards from the house of Mlle Martha who was expecting me for coffee.

'I saw you go past!' she exclaimed with a blush. 'It was splendid! You were going like the wind.'

'But I couldn't help myself going like the wind, Mademoiselle!'

'Oh! Exactly. *Ich liebe Gefahr!*' (I love danger).

She seemed to be beside herself with pleasure and I don't know what we said to each other next, but I do remember that as she placed the cup of coffee in front of me, she told me that today she had once again been obliged to beat a pupil.

When I returned on foot that evening, I was given the coolest of welcomes by the cadet. For the first time, I felt slightly sheepish in front of him. 'He thinks', I told myself, 'that you were frightened.' 'He thinks', an inner voice said to me, 'he thinks, quite correctly, that you were frightened.' No one made any allusion to my shameful jaunt.

I wish I were able to say that I suffered greatly from my humiliating experience, but I didn't. The world passed me by like a dream. One only woke from this dream at death. I would then see that I had been saved as my mother had promised. In the meantime, there was no point in bothering about what these earthly shadows said or did. One would have thought that this type of reasoning would put me at peace with myself. Not at all. Deep down inside me there was a destructive violence. If these shadows confronted or provoked me, I would feel bound to dispel them. There must be a contradiction there. I was a mass of contradictions even to myself.

The next day, I went out for a ride with the cadet, but this time I rode my own horse and not that creature that had been saddled and harnessed by Satan, and so nothing exceptional happened and I have not a single memory of what we talked about. However, no sooner were we back in the dining-room and before we had even taken off our boots and spurs, than we began to bicker. I don't know who began the quarrel, but I do remember that my friend looked even more handsome than usual, for he was one of those boys whose beauty is only revealed gradually. That afternoon he rather reminded me of a bright and frosty winter's day. In his most cutting voice, he quite rightly criticized me for not having taken my horse back to Oberlinxweiler myself on the previous evening instead of asking my orderly to do so, and he told me I lacked guts.

At this, my heart began to beat with happiness, for I knew that the moment had come for which I had been waiting for weeks. We stood there, a table separating us. In a quaking voice I asked him to take back what he had just said or I would knock him to the ground. Without moving, and with impressive calmness, he replied gently that he would do neither the one nor the other. So I walked to the other side of the table and grabbed him around the waist.

There is a sensuousness in anger. I had an extraordinary feeling of physical well-being and it seemed to me that my strength had increased tenfold. At last I was going to be able to smother my opponent like a bear crushing a man between his paws. The cadet looked astonished and was taken so much by surprise that it took him several seconds to recover. His steely body tossed and turned against mine as he tried to punch me in the face, but I had no difficulty pinning both his arms and in a sort of ecstasy I realized that I could do whatever I wanted with him. I slowly pushed him backwards, and we both lost our balance and fell down together, he with his back to the ground in such a way that his harder fall rather cushioned mine, and I found myself stretched bodily on top of him. Then I had the impression that he had suddenly given in, either because he was not as strong as I had thought, or because he no longer had any desire to fight. I pulled myself off him and sat astride his stomach, clenching his body tightly with my thighs; my hands still held his arms in a now useless grip. We both panted a bit, then I burst out laughing and said: 'And now who's lacking guts? Who's got his shoulders on the ground?'

His eyes were dark with rage. I waited another minute to savour my joy. I shook him roughly, but not angrily — my anger had vanished — and told him that if he did not want to be beaten up again, he should not push me to the limit. Little did I know that many years later both my play, *South*, and my novel, *Moïra*, would partly stem from this particular moment. The pleasure I experienced was so intense that I wanted to prolong it for ever. 'Say something!' I shouted with a laugh.

I could see from his eyes that he was searching for something to say and at last he uttered a phrase that was so full of hatred that I cannot bring myself to transcribe it, for it was unworthy of any man, especially a man such as he. What was the point of fighting? I had had what I wanted. I got to my feet and suggested to my friend that he brush himself down since Jarras might come in at any moment. I don't recall what happened next except that from that day the cadet addressed me in a completely different manner. The best in him came to the surface. Without ever being affable, he smiled at me more frequently and was less distant. Once his initial anger had passed, he bore no grudge. There was no pettiness in this troubled heart of his. When I think of him now, I am ready to acknowledge that in many ways he was an admirable human being and the fact is, that during these last weeks in Germany, I felt close to him and sought his company rather more than he sought mine.

A little while later, the lieutenant announced the arrival of the captain of our unit. I was told that he was a formidable character whose absence had been a blessing for all of us.

He was returning from a long leave and one day, in fact, a small, tubby man with yellow skin and a harsh, irritable voice appeared. One glance at him was enough to tell me that it would be sensible to ask to be demobbed. However, the officer in question paid hardly any attention to me and I could soon see that I was of no interest to him whatsoever. To tell the truth, he only had eyes for the other cadet, but there was something pitiless in his gaze which deeply astonished me. I seemed to be constantly observing these small dramas whose significance escaped me.

That evening, after dinner, the captain ensconced himself in his chair and, smiling at us like a carnivorous beast, told us that he was going to ask the cadet to produce his accounts. It was actually my friend's job to deal with our meals and look after the expenses. Fixing his cruel little eyes on him, the captain remarked in his nasal voice: 'He's so handsome that one hesitates to catch him out.' He rose to his feet, beckoned to the cadet to follow him, and the two left the room.

Some time went by. The lieutenant and the sub-lieutenant were talking to each other in a whisper and seemed thoroughly depressed. As for me, I kept quiet and leafed through one of my books. After a quarter of an hour, the cadet returned on his own with tears in his eyes. No questions were asked, but I had the feeling that I was not wanted and so I left the room.

Beyond all this, how many things must have been concealed from me. Exactly what those things were I did not want to know, but each time that I saw the captain I was filled with a feeling of indignation which he no doubt sensed. I regarded him as some sort of pacha who used my friend as his favourite whipping-boy. I doubt that I have ever found any man quite so immediately repugnant. I could not bear to think of him forcing tears from the cadet, whose rather arrogant pride, now I think about it, was that of a boy who felt weak and vulnerable. I had not understood that, but then how could I understand anything in the isolation that I had created for myself?

Since I had promised my father that I would stay for three months, I asked to be demobbed at the end of March. Spring that year was fairly mild and all over the Saar the landscape was starting to turn green. Small leaves could be seen in the hedges and crops began to sprout in the fields. The air felt wonderfully soft and at certain moments an indescribable joy would steal over me. I longed to laugh and roll in the grass again as once I used to. My heart seemed to be bursting with love, but who was it for? God? Most certainly, but I should also have liked to say those things you say when you are in love with a human being. But there was no one.

One day, the captain ordered me to saddle my horse because he wanted me to go for a ride with him. We set off. The horse I was riding was the one that I usually rode and, since he and I knew each other well, I had no need to dread any surprises. With loud cracks of his whip, the captain shot off into the woods. I must admit that he had a marvellous seat, and as he galloped, he sang as loudly as he could in his nasal voice. Riding hell for leather, I followed this fat little man closely enough to be able to hear him call out from time to time:

'Are you there, cadet?'

'I'm right behind you', I replied.

'Right behind you, *sir*' he said in his nasal whine.

'Certainly, sir' I answered in a fury. I tried to overtake him, but he indicated that I should stay behind.

Because my heart was beating madly and I felt as if I was

suffocating, all I retain from that crazy gallop is an overriding feeling of physical excitement, but mixed with it is a sort of satisfaction I find hard to describe, a violent sense of well-being.

I have no idea what the captain had in mind making me gallop through the woods. Had he heard rumours about my escapade with the stallion from Hell? It is possible. I don't think he cared very much for me and he perceived an innocence in me that he reckoned was ridiculous and undignified. Be that as it may, I, for my part, perceived a carnal gluttony in him that I judged equally severely. We were born to disagree. I was nevertheless delighted to have shown him that I was perfectly at home in the saddle. It was the only time we went out riding together.

Once more there is a gap in my memory and all of a sudden I see myself in a room in the house in which the cadet lived at the other end of the village, not in solitude like me, but surrounded with neighbouring houses. The room is large and well heated, and seems very pleasant with its big, peasant furniture and the brightly coloured holy pictures on the walls. There is an enormous wardrobe, a bed in an alcove and, on the left, a half-open door through which I notice a young woman who is wiping the tears from her eyes. This door closes again and, close by me, the lieutenant and the sub-lieutenant are speaking in low voices to my friend who is bowing his head rather sadly. It is obvious that something is wrong, but I detach myself and keep silent. What time can it be? At my feet the sun shines over the grey floor. There is a hum of voices, then I catch these words spoken by the cadet: 'She says it upsets her because of her husband.' There is a further buzz of questions and advice, then comes the rather melancholy voice of the cadet again: 'Yesterday evening, she allowed me to let down her hair. It's very thick, and so heavy . . . ' 'Adulterer', I say to myself. The cadet is half seated on a table and his head keeps dropping even lower. I could see he was suffering: he was madly in love . . .

I hardly ever went into this room, but it was so attractive and charming that I could not help saying to myself: 'When he looks round the room, he probably loathes these walls and this furniture, because this is the place where he is so unhappy.' I gradually came to realize that the cadet was sick with desire. This would explain his strange behaviour. I suspected that when we had grappled in the dining-room, he had allowed himself to be thrown to the ground out of despair. He was surely stronger than me, but he was made of steel, and steel sometimes cracks.

One night when the moon was full, he and I found ourselves in this same room with two girls sitting beside us. Who were these women and what on earth was I doing there? I don't know the answers to these questions, but the fact is that I was in a room lit only by the light of the moon, talking to one of the girls while my friend was kissing the other. What a very strange scene. Something which Mlle Martha had said to me kept coming to my mind: '*Wir sind nicht die echten Deutschen. Die echten Deutschen sind in Berlin.*' (We are not real Germans. The real Germans are in Berlin). The girl I was with was speaking about my eyes (she was paying me a compliment and I never did forget a compliment, did I?): 'Just now, you were looking towards the window and I noticed your eyes. *Es war ein Licht darin.*' (There was a light in them.) She was very kind, but I was not attracted to her at all. My friend had chosen the prettier one. I don't know how I managed to get away, but I am certain that I did not linger long. I was particularly struck by the fact that both these girls were strapped into their blouses as if they were suits of armour. With Lola, it was easier.

He wanted to corrupt me, I thought when I was alone. Isn't he frightened of getting some disease? The memory of my Uncle Willie kept coming back to me from time to time. It was clear, nevertheless, that I was changing. Springtime affected me in the most classic manner. I was quite taken aback. For a long time, I had not thought about such desires for they no longer conformed to the extraordinary notion that I had of myself.

At last there was a reply to my request to be demobbed, and on the morning of the feast of the Annunciation, I caught the train at Neunkirchen station. I have not even the slightest recollection of whether I said good-bye to anyone.

I returned to Paris on 26 March 1919, but I did not find my father at home because he had gone to Copenhagen where he had some business to attend to. It is thanks to the letters he wrote to me while he was away that I can date certain minor events. My sister Anne, who I was delighted to see again, gave me fifty francs pocket money from my father and reminded me that it should cover all my expenditure for a month.

I was deliriously happy. There was a marvellous sweetness in the air and the chestnut trees in the Avenue Henri-Martin were covered in tiny new leaves. For no particular reason, I started to run through the streets. No one ever beat me at running, but who was there to race against? All my old friends were working at the times I went on my long walks. One of the first visits I paid was to our neighbours, the nuns. I went to call on the reverend mothers in their sombre visiting rooms where they laughed and joked about everything with me, even if they did slip in the occasional serious remark about the great evils of the world, and the judgement that awaits us all. I would then become even more earnest than they were and I would peer desperately past the thick wooden grills through which I could only see a part of their faces. In a low voice, Mother Marie-Adolphine, the Mother Superior, and Mother Marie-Joachim, the novice mistress, reminded me of the great honour God was bestowing on me by granting me a vocation. I left them to attend benediction in the chapel and once more I revelled in that music which spoke to me of the true kingdom, beyond the visible world. What delighted me was the fact that this chapel never changed. Whether I was there or not, whether it was wartime or peacetime, there were always nuns kneeling before the Blessed Sacrament. And so everything was in order. I was saved. Everyone was saved. I doubt if I was ever more light-hearted than during that last week in March 1919. Peace, peace at last! The nightmare was gone forever. We could laugh again. There was going to be the greatest Fourteenth of July celebration ever.

I ran about Paris in a sort of drunken state, for I felt she was my city and she belonged to me because I was born there. Because I was so eager to learn, I could always be seen with a book under my arm. Sometimes it would be a guide to old Paris, in the margins of which I would make pencil drawings of architectural details. I was fascinated by all the old houses. I would push open the *porte-cochères* to glimpse the courtyards and I would climb the staircases when the concièrges were not watching. Sometimes I would carry my copy of Virgil or a volume of Montaigne in the Costes edition. One day when I was travelling on the No.19 tram and absorbed in my reading, a young woman — we were alone — was looking at me so intensely that I glanced up. She had a lovely face, pale and serious, and when I smiled at her, she asked me whether I was reading the gospel. This unusual question led me to believe that I must have had a rather wise expression. I replied that no, I was reading Montaigne, at which she smiled back and there our conversation ended.

I probably had a fairly tranquil air about me, but so many things were now stirring inside me! I had begun to look at myself in mirrors again, for there were many around Paris. What became of my religion in all this? Well, we shall see.

The nuns from the Rue Cortambert had every reason to speak to me about the evils of the world, for I was dazzled by its dangerous beauty. Certainly everything looked resplendent in this month of April when the doors were thrown wide open to greet a resurrection of mankind. This was the way I saw things. Since I hardly ever read the newspapers, I knew nothing about the riots which were taking place virtually everywhere. I remember that before falling asleep each night, I would sometimes laugh out loud for no reason at all, except for the fact that I was alive. This rather muddled sort of happiness sometimes reached such a level of intensity that it resembled suffering. I didn't know what it was I wanted. By day, I would write poems and stories, one of which remains in my memory. I called it 'Jean-Sebastien'; this double name referred to two young men who shared the same room and when, for whatever reason, they had to part, even for an hour, they would be so overcome with worry and anxiety that they would start to panic and would run around the streets in terror until they were reunited. The streets, the fear that stalked the pavements, the way the heart would leap with joy; I described these things with the passion that was born of innocence, for the real significance of all this was completely hidden from me.

I would also sketch short scenes depicting fear or violence. A murdered man whose body lay in front of a huge log fire. Someone is making his way cautiously down a staircase, with a lighted candle in his hand, and looking over his shoulder because he is frightened of a person who is following him. This drawing was entitled 'Followed' and it disturbed me to look at it. I never drew anything improper. I doubt that I would have been able to do so.

Was it at this time that I first heard Beethoven's Ninth Symphony? It seems to me now that it must have been, even though in my notes for 1939 I say that it was at the end of the war. When I think about it, it could not have been in 1918, for I was in mufti when I heard the concert in question. I had handed in my khaki uniform at the end of June and replaced it with the sky-blue uniform in early September that year, and it is most unlikely that the concert would have been given in July or August. There is no doubt that early April of 1919 would seem the most likely time. My confusion may arise from the fact that in 1939, in the huge hall of the Trocadero, I also remember seeing a large number of soldiers in uniform, and among them a number of wounded who were convalescing. In any case, this concert made an indelible impression on me. Until I heard it reach the heights that Beethoven attained, I scarcely knew what orchestral music could be like. When, out of the vast silence, I heard those amazing murmured notes that introduced the allegro, my concentration grew so intense that my entire fate might have been at stake. It was as if I were watching an eagle beating the air with its powerful wings as it wheeled above a chasm. Whole new areas opened to my imagination. This majestic music transported me and spoke to me in a language I did not know. It seemed to me to be religious, but not in a way I was used to. It was as if I was standing at the centre of a storm feeling alternatively delighted or terrified depending on the tempo. There was more to the world than the reassuring voice of the Church, the universe was larger than I had thought. The Faith was certainly not in question, but its horizons drew back and lost themselves in areas that the catechism had not foreseen. Everything was so much more vast, so much darker and so much more attractive. Had I been better informed about my religion, I would have understood that behind every mystery lies another, but within the tumultuous magic of sound, I had the sense that an equilibrium which I had imagined was fixed for all time had been broken, and it produced a shock from which I took some time to recover. My anxiety was mixed with a strange feeling of exultation. All of a sudden, I was far away from the world of the nuns, their white serge habits and their Latin hymns, yet God was still present in this music in which one seemed to hear the voice of mankind itself, and God was also there in the joy of the frenetic final movement. I left the concert hall quite overcome, rather like a prisoner released from prison who doesn't know what to do with his freedom because it frightens him.

This great emotional experience was to mark me more deeply than I realized. Nevertheless, I calmed myself. Gently, like a grandmother watching over a child, the course of daily life gradually allowed everything to fall into place. From time to time, the memory of that huge shout of 'Joy!' would ring out in my head again, but within the walls of the dark little room where I spent my life, the surge of excitement would soon vanish.

Ted sometimes came to call on us and once more I would begin to suffer in a way that I could not understand. I burned. By that I mean that the whole front part of my body ached with an unbearable desire. I laughed and looked at the young sailor's face, taking care not to lower my gaze. The discomfort I felt was acute and in the end it was such agony that I would try to avoid him, while he, by some cruel irony, would purposely seek out my company on the pretext of wanting to discuss philosophical problems. He insisted on making me go on long walks with him, and I found his conversation extremely boring, but how could I not fail to notice his ivory skin and the perfect round column of his neck?

I ought to say that when Ted was not there I felt perfectly happy and thought no more about him. Something was nevertheless troubling my heart and who was there who could explain why? I knew no priest in Paris. Father Crété was away. He called on my father at the beginning of March and I imagine it was in order to discuss me and my vocation. For the moment, he was far away and, besides, what could I have told him? An angel would have been needed to interrogate me. I was not conscious of any sin, except one which I had committed at Oberlinxweiler and I had already confessed that, but the world struck me as being far too desirable. There was far too much light, too much liberty, too much joy both on earth and in my soul. I cannot remember the date on which Easter fell that year, but it must have been at the beginning of April because the offices of Holy Week were said in the crypt at the Rue Cortambert, and it was there that I heard Mass. On the ninth of April, as I walked up the stairs from this crypt, I decided to go home and write an important letter to my father.

Walking up the stairs from that dark crypt . . . My God, whatever went on in my soul that day, while I climbed those stone steps and came out into a street blazing with sunshine, and a sky the colour of triumphal blue? Something inside me had suddenly changed. I could no longer accept the idea of detaching myself from the world and an enormous weight fell from my shoulders: the entire weight of a cross. It was not a revolt, it was desertion, and the cross would return, much later and much heavier, for we all have our crosses . . .

Was there a debate, at least? Yes, certainly. So great was the wrench I felt as I climbed the steps of that stone staircase that I thought I was going to die. It would kill me to renounce the world, but by the world I meant the creation, the freedom to come and go on this earth, not the dangerous affairs of mankind, not sin, for the world for me was the heavenly light that shone on my face, in the woods, in the streets and wherever my fancy took me. There was no question of renouncing God, but I was searching for a middle path, one which is neither narrow nor wide, one that does not exist, for it is merely the wider path which the devil allows us to mistake for the narrow one — a *reasonable* narrow path. Oh! God, what an overpowering sense of joy took possession of me as I returned to our little provincial street, with its quiet houses and small gardens.

One should tell the whole truth. I was thoughtless enough to write to my father to say that I had changed my mind, that I no longer wished to become a monk, but simply a priest. Simply a priest . . . My excuse is that I did not know what I was saying. I also wrote to our friend the American nun who, knowing that we were poor, had offered to pay my dowry. (I don't believe I have mentioned that the nun in question, Roselys*, was now living at a convent in Angers under the name of Mother Francis of Assisi). Finally and very carefully, I wrote to Father Crété. Then I waited for their replies. I have my father's in front of me. He told me that he had never been opposed to any of my plans, even though he had felt bitterly upset when I announced that I wished to leave the secular world. As far as my vocation to the priesthood was concerned, he was of the opinion that I should wait a little longer, and he advised me to spend a few years at a university in the American South, where a place had been reserved for me. I have forgotten what Roselys said to me. I have a recollection of a rather melancholy letter, but there were no useless reproaches and she was certainly very tactful. As to Father Crété's letter, alas! I no longer have it, but certain words that I believe he used have remained with me: 'My child, allow me to address you as such, for how could I write to you otherwise? . . . The mystery of human freedom . . . Like that poor La Mennais* . . . ' (This letter was later found, in 1972. The quotations are exact.) I was shattered. These almost indecipherable phrases filled me with horror. Was it at this moment, or later, or even earlier, when he gave me to understand that he questioned my sanity? The word resounded within me like a stone thrown into a chasm. A part of my life has been spent in ridding my soul of the terrifying thoughts that his opinion aroused in me.

* See *The Green Paradise*
* Abbé La Mennais (1782–1854). French priest who lost his faith. Translator of *The Imitation of Christ* and *The Divine Comedy*. (*Tr.*)

Far be it from me to judge a man who was superior to me in every way, but I do believe that if he had wanted to point me in the direction of despair, he would not have behaved differently.

I pulled myself together, however. My zest for life was so strong that having touched ground I bounced back like a ball at once. The world was mine. I was eighteen and I had a few francs in my pocket; if I wanted to turn right, I would turn right; if I wanted to turn left, I would turn left, and as I walked along the banks of the Seine in the April sunshine, I started to sing to myself again. I would not go to the Isle of Wight. I was free. Who could say whether my decision was correct or not? After years of reflection, I am still not sure. Certainly, I did nothing that was wrong. Every morning I attended the seven o'clock Mass and I went to daily communion. The rest of the time, I wrote what I called stories or poems, or I roamed around Paris on foot, having long ago spent my fifty francs. And how had I spent them? On the *quais* where I bought second-hand books. Which books?

Here, I feel obliged to mention something that may seem strange. It was the fine seventeenth- and eighteenth-century leather-bound volumes with their gold fleurons and their blue and pale pink marbled fly-leaves that particularly appealed to me. One could buy several of them at the time for only a few pence and I did not realize that I was building myself a library of books that are now extremely rare, although I never bought anything without having first glanced through a few pages, and I almost always chose religious works (those which no one else wanted, those which cluttered the barrows, the same sort of books that the Abbé Bremond* was probably looking for at the same

* Henri Bremond (1865–1933). Controversial French critic and

period). There were some which I discarded because a voice seemed to be warning me that they might cause me to go back on my recent decision and make me quit this world for good. What voice? I don't know, but I realized much later that these books came from the library of Port-Royal. One could recognize the tone: something totally uncompromising and intimidating which disturbed the sinner in me who had not yet been informed that he was corrupt, to use the language of those austere gentlemen. I put the books back in their box and replaced them with others that were rather more appealing. What had happened? Why was there no one who could speak to me? The brief advice I was given at confession hardly clarified anything and I no longer had my own confessor. I didn't want to be instructed by Father Crété and, besides, he was far away and I had the feeling that he had abandoned me for good.

One day, however, I saw him again at the foot of the staircase that led to the chapel in the Rue Cortambert. I was coming out of the chapel and there he was. He said a few words and smiled at me with that look of kindness that made him an angel in my eyes, and he then said: 'Remember, my child: *oportet eum crescere, me autem minui*'. I believe these may have been the last words I heard him speak in this world, for I remember nothing else apart from the fact that it was a beautiful day and that he stood there in the light, by the entrance, with his finger raised, rather as if he were an apparition.

I suffered even more anguish than these pages may suggest. Even if I thought otherwise today, the proof that I was wrong lies in front of me, for I wrote a great deal. I have

theologian, and a Jesuit priest for twenty-two years. (*Tr.*)

forgotten to say that, having taken the first part of the baccalauréat in 1917, I was keen to take the second as soon as I could. To this end, I took the books I needed with me to the Argonne, then to the Veneto and then to Germany. I carted around two fat books of philosophy which bored me to death, as well as books on physics, chemistry and mathematics, subjects about which I understood nothing. Philosophy struck me as useless, since the essentials of knowledge could be found in the Bible which contained all wisdom. Above all, I was appalled at the different systems which contradicted each other without ever reaching a mutually acceptable conclusion. Philosophers such as John Stuart Mill and Auguste Comte allowed such hateful choices that to my mind they were more repellent than the others. How comforting I found it to go back to my Crampon translation which I was to write so unjustly about later!

Back in Paris in March 1919, I lost my head at first because I was free again; then in April came the religious crisis I mentioned and also those immensely long walks when I dreamed and sang to myself, before I eventually pulled myself together and decided to take my baccalauréat in July. No more laughing, I then said to myself, and I drew up an amazingly rigorous time-table. Here it is: *Morning*: 6.00 - 7.00a.m., history; 8.30 - 9.30a.m., chemistry; 9.30 - 10.30a.m., natural history; 11.00 - 12.00p.m., physics; 12.00 - 12.30p.m., geography. *Afternoon*: 1.30 - 2.30p.m., philosophy; 3.00 - 4.00p.m., chemistry; 4.30 - 5.00p.m., history; 5.30 - 7.30p.m., essay; 8.30 - 10.30p.m., philosophy.

I wonder how I found the time to read Pascal. Yet I did read him. From 1919 to 1935, I noted down everything I read, and in June 1919 I definitely read the *Pensées*, going down on my knees when I came to the *Mystère de Jesus*, but either I am badly mistaken, or else I gave up this inhuman schedule after a few weeks. For I also read Montaigne and — what an appalling jumble — Edgar Allen Poe, Tolstoy, Bergson, Ibsen and Verhaeren. As the date of the baccalauréat approached, I fell into a sort of calm despair, for I knew that something like a miracle would be needed to make me pass, although deep down, it did not matter very much to me since no one had asked me to take this exam and I think I only did it to please my father. At last the dreaded date I had been waiting for arrived. I was alone at home. Anne went out virtually every day and my father, much against his own wishes, was obliged to stay longer in Denmark.

My memory of those two days at the Sorbonne is like an unpleasant dream. I kept telling myself that everything I wrote or answered was untrue. My French and English essays elicited some favourable comments but a dismal silence hung over my written replies to the very strange questions about the irregular behaviour of the sunflower and the caprices of the laws of gravity. Time went by — but surely I had not passed in anything. That, in any case, was the impression I had when I cast a disillusioned eye over the list of successful candidates. I looked at this list, which was pinned up in a corridor of the Sorbonne, from a distance, for the idea of pushing into the crowd and being touched by these boys who were shoving each other to look at a little sheet of paper repelled me, and in my own mind I was convinced I had not passed anyway. It must seem inconceivable that I did not insist on finding out, that I did not wait, but I was probably too proud to want to have proof of my failure. I did not want to know about that sort of truth. I preferred to return home saying to myself: 'I've almost certainly failed, but who knows?' And then, perhaps none of this was real. My personal system of philosophy allowed me to question the very fact. It was very convenient, after all. It kept the peace. I remember that it was a fine day and that as I walked along the Avenue Henri-Martin I noticed the huge green branches of the chestnut trees that rustled softly in the breeze and seemed to bless my indifference. I wrote to tell my father that I had failed and he replied that it did not matter and that I had not exactly been through the ideal conditions in which to take an exam. Twenty-seven years later, my friend Philippe who had been with me at the time (although I had deserted him, not wishing to find out), asserts that I did pass. It would be strange if that were true, but I do not really believe it.

Whatever I had done, I would not be able to remember everything. If only I had kept a diary at the time . . . Actually, I did keep one, but it was too irregular and only fragments of it remain. The inconvenience of a diary is that it takes the place of the memory and deprives it of much of its freshness. In the end one only remembers the words one has written. That is what will happen to me when I have finished recounting my story. There will, at least, be this book.

My cousin Sarah would sometimes boast of having a Protestant bishop for a grandfather. She no more resembled the '*filles*' of today than she did the young ladies of 1919, even the most emancipated of them. She had a heart of gold, a fiery temperament, eager to please, as frivolous as can be, religious, yet a bit sentimental: that is more or less how she appears to me in my memory. Once, when she was making caramels yet again, something induced me to tell her about my strange adventure with Lola. Perhaps I wanted to get it off my conscience, for I had always felt guilty about it. On the other hand, I could not have known much about my cousin for, to my astonishment, without putting down the long wooden spoon with which she was rhythmically stirring her pot (there was something almost religious in the care with which she made her confections), she said to me: 'What a shame you didn't go back to see her. It would have been *so wonderful* . . . ' These words, which I have emphasized, took my breath away. I retorted that it would have been a sin, and a serious one. 'No doubt, no doubt, said the bishop's granddaughter. 'All the same . . . ' A little while later, she told me that she was going to go away on a short trip with Ted the sailor, but that I was not to say a word about it in my letters to Uncle Edward. I promised. They were going to go to Le Croisic. I did not know this part of the country. I imagined them walking by the sea and eating at open air cafés, but I did not envy them in the least, for I loathed the sea. What an extraordinary idea to go down there! It never occurred to me for a moment that there could be anything besides sea walks and cafés. If Ted wanted to go far away from Paris, that suited me perfectly, for, as I have mentioned already, I found him boring, and then there was also this burning sensation that I experienced whenever he appeared . . .

After a week or ten days my cousin returned. She seemed very satisfied with her trip, told me how wonderful she found Ted's company and somehow succeeded in questioning me about what I thought of this jaunt. She must have worried in case I said something wicked, for my innocence alarmed her. Why should she want to know what I thought about her trip? I did not think anything of it particularly.

'You're not to start imagining things . . . '

'What things, cousin Sarah?'

She told me that men often tried to have their way with women, or they tried to . . .

'Not him!' I protested. 'He's far too sensible. He'd never do anything wicked.'

This particular phrase has remained in my mind because it reflects the depths of my ignorance. Could anyone be more foolish, more naïve? In any case, my cousin appeared to be comforted, and it can never have occurred to her that what I should have said was that if he had not tried to have his way, as she put it, then it was definitely because *she* was too sensible ever to do anything wicked. She suddenly burst out laughing, threw her arms round my neck and said: 'When Ted hears what you said he'll be so pleased. He's very fond of you, you know.' I did not understand why she was so happy. I still seem to be able to hear that young American speaking about me to my cousin: 'He's just a kid!' Both of them have been dead for a long time. Little did I then suspect the suffering that would await me in a few months' time.

One day in May, in circumstances that escape me now, my friend Philippe took me to the top floor of the apartment block where he lived with his parents. We found ourselves in a maid's room which was in rather a mess. Why had he taken me there? I have no idea, but I asked him suddenly:

'Where does one find women?'

He roared with laughter. 'All over the place. In the street. At the Sphinx (he explained what the Sphinx was). Outside theatres, inside theatres. You've got to watch for them and know what to say, and so on.'

I asked him whether one had to offer them money to do the things I wanted them to do.

'It depends. If you've got the gift of the gab, you can get

off lightly, but it's best to have a bit of money on one for drinks.'

I did not know whether I had the gift of the gab or not. As for money, I was quite sure I had none at all.

But what did I want then? Through my lack of experience, I did not know exactly what it was. I imagined superhuman delights, such as the gods must have known, for it was my great misfortune to have become interested in mythology, and I was quite carried away by the subject. Among the books at home, was Beauzée's little *Dictionnaire de la Fable*, which, in its slightly flat and outdated style, recounted all the love affairs of those overexcited divinities with which the Greek genius has filled our universe. There was plenty that was beyond me. There were a number of anomalies which remained incomprehensible to me because the author only alluded to them in somewhat polite and obscure terms, but I concluded from my almost habitual reading that sensuality opened some kind of heavenly gate to man through which anyone could enter. So, why not me? A simple country priest would have explained to me in a couple of minutes that I was prey to delusions, but there was no one I could speak to. This is what strikes me particularly about this period in my life: I was alone. No doubt I went to confession whenever I had committed a sin, but the need for communion had deserted me, even though I went to Mass every Sunday. Religion, it seems, had little effect. Like the poet, I was haunted, and all the more seriously while my unrequited passion remained purely cerebral.

Now that I had taken, or failed, my baccalauréat, I had a sense of total freedom and I did not worry at all about the future. Almost every day I went to the Louvre. To my mind, there was scarcely any danger for me in the gallery that ran alongside the river for there was nothing there that was particularly voluptuous. I could not say the same for the antique sculpture rooms which I only entered with a guilty conscience. Why was this? Did not my mother used to take us there? It was all rather different now. I imagined these naked men and women leading suspect lives. Their nudity alone was a sin in my eyes. It really was not right to look at them, to gaze at them for too long or too curiously. How fiercely my heart would beat as I walked amongst these marble statues and looked up at them! They hurt me and brought on that burning feeling throughout the front part of my body that I had begun to experience without knowing the reason. These gods were impassive, but how they made one suffer, and yet what a curious pleasure there was in this suffering. It was painful and yet one did not want the pain to stop. You turned away from them and they drew you back. You were frightened of being seen looking at these people and you had to wait for a propitious moment . . . Now, go now, there's no one there, you can revel and suffer once more, be possessed and captivated. It may all be stone but it's still fascinating. Admire and learn, intoxicate yourself, wide-eyed boy lost in the cavernous gloom of this sinister Olympia!

In the courtyard of the Louvre and later along the *quais*, I found myself overcome with an inexplicable sense of sadness. My throat and intestines had seized up. I did not know what I wanted, or rather, I wanted those things that only existed in my imagination. My erotic dreams took no account of the humanity that could be seen in the streets. I remember sitting on a bench by the river outside the Louvre feeling truly depressed at the thought that human beings were not gods.

It was about this time that one day I heard from my friend the cadet who asked if he could come to see me.

What would I not give for a slightly clearer memory of those months that mattered so much to me! But I can only manage to summon up brief, isolated scenes like those very modern galleries where huge spaces separate the pictures. So, here I am in the Avenue du Bois with the blond cadet. My impression is that he is still wearing a uniform. In any case, I can see his fine, pure face with those *virginal* blue eyes (is that why I only ever see him dressed in sky-blue?). As for me, I was wearing a suit made from tiny black and white check cloth which probably looked very elegant when it was worn by my brother-in-law, but which fitted me rather badly, despite the fact that it had been altered, making me look like one of those men who frequent race courses, and totally out of keeping with the expression I wore; I loathed this suit with the same hatred I once had for the overcoat with the astrakhan collar I wore as a boy.

After quite a long walk, about which I recall absolutely nothing, we eventually reached the Porte Dauphine and continued as far as the Avenue Bugeaud. It was there that I told the blond cadet that I had changed my ideas and had now decided to have some fun.

'Have some fun?'

'Yes, with women.'

He then asked me a question I had not expected. 'How are you going to manage that?'

I laughed and told him that I knew very well what one had to do to find women. He gave me a solemn look. He was much calmer than he had been in Germany. I expect his lusty cravings had been assuaged in Paris. In any case, he let me laugh for a few seconds and then said with a melancholy smile: 'I preferred you the way you were in

Germany.' I did not know what to reply to that, or if I did I have forgotten, but I was astonished to hear him speak as if on someone else's behalf and I felt suddenly guilty.

We parted and were never to see each other again. After a few hours, I thought no more about him and the desire to have fun returned again, but where and how did one find women? This use of the plural was important. That is what people used to say. I remembered that Philippe had told me that you could find them at theatres but that you had to have some money for drinks. With this in mind, I decided to have a go and to sell the signet ring I wore on my left hand. This ring (it had no crest) had been given to me by a friend of my father's when I was fifteen years old and I had never taken it off. I cherished it more than anyone could imagine. Firstly, it belonged to me and that alone gave it an exceptional quality, and then everyone knew that gold was the most precious metal in the world. It used to give me a strange pleasure to slide the ring up and down my finger. It seemed to me to be so much a part of myself that I would sometimes even rub it against my lips. Despite all this, I resolved to make a sacrifice, reckoning that the carnal pleasures I was about to discover would surely be compensation enough. I set off — can I ever forget it? — to the little jeweller's shop in the Rue Guichard, a few minutes from where we lived, and I showed the man the ring in question. He examined it with a disdainful expression, as if he was tired of examining signet rings, and gave it back to me saying: 'Twenty francs.'

Twenty francs . . . I wondered whether that was enough to have a woman. After some hesitation, for I was a bit disappointed in the offer and it never occurred to me that the man might not be honest, I agreed and I left the wretched shop without my signet ring but with a twenty franc note in my wallet.

Then I had to choose which theatre. Since I was alone in the house, I could do as I pleased. I scrutinized the list of plays in the *Journal* and I think that eventually I selected the Palais-Royal because I had heard my parents say it was a theatre in which children should never set foot. What play were they showing? I don't remember.

Already petrified, I presented myself at the box office a good hour before the show started and bought a seat in the balcony. The auditorium was empty. *They* had not arrived yet. Gradually, a few did appear, although they were all accompanied, which did not simplify matters. At last the theatre filled up and the curtain rose on a play that seemed terribly obscure to me; never having seen any plays except those put on at the Châtelet, which were very straightfor-ward, I was not able to appreciate how the characters related to one another, although I did come to realize that several of them were obsessed with the same yearning as me: how to go to bed with a woman. I remember there was one scene towards the middle of the second act in which a fat lady asked a girl to sing to her, and the girl, who was young and pretty (she would do for me, I thought), began to sing a song full of innuendo which, with the single exception of one person who did not understand the allusions, had the whole audience roaring with laughter. Then the fat lady, who had probably not understood the song either, clapped her hands and said: 'I adore these simple little songs'.

During the intervals I wandered about the corridors and in front of the theatre, hoping that some charming girl would smile at me, but nothing of the kind occurred. No one took any notice of me and the cadet's question came back to my mind: 'How are you going to manage that?' It appeared that Philippe's instructions were incorrect. I returned home the way I had come, yet I was so carefree that all the way along the riding track on the Avenue Henri-Martin, I sang to myself. Nevertheless, I missed my fine ring and wondered what I was going to say to my father when he came back from Denmark. With the money that remained, I bought a few books on the *quais*. As for the desire to have fun, it suddenly left me, at least for a while: it really was too difficult. Perhaps it would have been easier, I told myself, to go to that place called the Sphinx, but I would have been terrified. There was the real difficulty: I lacked daring. Someone only had to look at me and I blushed.

What I am about to say may be rather surprising. In spite of the fact that my mind was filled with ideas of debauchery, I was still just as pious and the Bible was still my principal reading. I always had in my pocket a slim volume that Mouser had given me, handsomely bound in calf, which contained English translations of Ecclesiastes, the Book of Job and St James's epistle. Why this choice? Mouser had made it herself.

It corresponded to her own ideas. She liked anything that was high-minded, gloomy and depressing. This same volume, which I have always kept, incidentally, and is still on my bedside table, also included the Book of Proverbs which is well known for being extremely strict on the question of fools and disobedient children who should be punished mercilessly. I was not too keen on the Proverbs, but I liked Job, particularly the obscure passages. Whenever I felt weary on my treks across Paris, I would sit down on a bench and read Job. I believe I would do the same today if it were still possible to read in the streets of Paris. One day

I decided to sit down on a bench in the Boulevard de la Madeleine. In 1919 you could do that. The traffic hardly bothered me. It was far less dense and the air was not yet polluted.

If I remember this detail, it is because of what followed. It must have been eleven o'clock in the morning. Having finished my reading, I put the book back in my pocket and went to have a look in the window of Conard's bookshop which was then situated near the statue of Jules Simon (this abomination has now been resited near the church of Saint-Augustin; Conard's bookshop is somewhere else). As I was gazing at the books, I heard an extremely polite voice saying to me: 'Excuse me'. Turning round, I saw a very elegantly dressed young man who was doffing his hat and smiling at me. His handsome face had been lightly powdered and I looked at him with amazement for I did not know him. With a smile that revealed all his teeth, he asked me the time. 'But look over there, monsieur', I said, pointing to the clock just in front of the Madeleine. With another smile he nodded and, doffing his hat again, he departed. It was then that I noticed that he wore peach-coloured gaiters and carried a walking-stick. Why, I wondered, should he have asked me such a stupid question? Had he not seen the clock? Was he making fun of me? Yet he seemed so polite. The pale hat, the gaiters, that walking-stick . . . What elegance! He must have thought me very poorly dressed . . . After a moment I gave the matter no further thought, but I remembered it much later on.

When my father returned from Denmark towards the end of July that year, he told me that he had received a letter from my Uncle Walter that concerned me. Anne was also there, and we heard that Uncle Walter had offered to take charge of me for four years should I wish to complete my studies at an American university.

'So what will you do, Papa?' asked Anne.

'Send him off packing.'

His answer came like a blow to the heart. On no account did I wish to leave France, which I loved, for a country which I did not know. What is more, I considered myself French, yet how could I possibly disobey my father? That was the last thing I intended doing. He could have sent me to Timbuctoo and I would have agreed. So I ventured no opinion and simply said 'All right' as I always did. In retrospect, I congratulate myself not only for having always obeyed him promptly and without argument, but also for accepting one of the unique opportunities life has offered me.

However, that was not how I saw matters at that time. I behaved like a man condemned to death. My father told me that he would ask my uncle to send me to the University of Virginia, which was the best in the South, and once again I said 'all right'. I knew that my father had no money. What I did not know and only discovered much later, was that he earned a great deal, but these considerable sums were mainly used to pay off debts, some of which dated back to the early years of the century. In fact, before the war, anxious about leaving us all enough to live on, he had speculated, lost, speculated further and lost again, each time borrowing sums of money which added together amounted to a fortune. This wise, scrupulous and very modest man had such faith in the streak of luck which would solve everything. By the time he stopped speculating, he was practically ruined. He had to work for fifteen years to pay everyone back and though he died without owing a penny to anyone, he left us without even enough to pay for his burial.

One can understand his delight when he learnt that my uncle was going to look after me. But in any case, had not my father taken good care of his niece Sarah for nine years? Sarah, who was an orphan and who my uncle did not know what to do with when he sent her to us in 1910 asking my parents to look after her for a few weeks. In all this I cannot help noticing an element of give and take though it does not in any way diminish my uncle's generosity.

Have I mentioned that towards the end of the war, Sarah had also joined the Red Cross? Her work, which was far less onerous than Anne's or Retta's, consisted in comforting the wounded at the American hospital in Neuilly. Her stories were brimful with platefuls of *patisserie* and 'absolutely adorable doctors, my dear'. But enough of that. In 1919, by a fortunate coincidence, the American Red Cross offered all its members free repatriation on a boat which the French government would put at their disposition. My father decided that Sarah should return home. And why should not Julian, who had also served with the American Red Cross, make use of this opportunity? Why not, indeed? said the Red Cross. The ship was due to leave Marseilles on 19 September. I would be a little late for the beginning of the course, 'but I am confident that this boy will catch everybody up', said my father.

Flabbergasted, I murmured: 'All right', before setting off immediately to announce the appalling news to my friend Paul, whom I have purposely not mentioned yet because I'm not sure it would please him. Suffice it to say that he was extremely left wing, a '*kienthalien*', was what people said at the lycée during the war; Paul had very rigid views which he expressed unsparingly. He listened to me, then said forcefully: 'You have to rebel'. Rebel against Papa! I told him it was impossible and he gave me a look of scorn.

Bring back those golden days when I imagined myself to

be so unhappy! I poured out my troubles to the confidant I have called Paul, and I spoke to him like someone who was going into exile for ever to die in a hostile land. I entrusted to him, as if he were the one friend I had in this world, my few, deeply treasured art books. Suddenly, I detested America. My true homeland was France; I was being taken away from France, from the city that was my home.

After a few hours, I calmed down and with one of those extraordinary fluctuations of mood which formed the basis of my character at the time, I took a certain pleasure in seeing everything from a romantic point of view. After all, there was Chateaubriand. I remembered *Atala*. In the small drawing-room at the Rue Cortambert, I made faces and preened myself in front of the mirror, and I imagined that over there I would be admired and loved since that was what I most desired. I tried desperately to reassure myself, which may explain my perpetual craving for flattery.

So as to accustom myself to the idea of this country I did not know, I used to play ragtime records I would never normally have listened to, on our gramophone. What a gulf separated Chopin and ragtime! I found this modern music barbaric, and yet at moments there were tunes that would make me suddenly want to cry, although I have to admit that at the time I cried very easily and not without a certain secret pleasure. I was probably listening to the very first Gershwin tunes.

Today, I wonder how I could have been so naïve for such a long time. In order to appreciate the American way of life, it seemed indispensable to read Edgar Allan Poe. I went to Galignani's bookshop and with the money that my father had given me for my nineteenth birthday I bought the complete works of the great visionary writer. 'Besides', I thought, 'it will be good for my English.' I read him, and, as might be expected, my eyes popped out of my head. These stories about people being buried alive, about the dead being brought back to life while protesting that they were dead, about castles haunted by a plague, all those extravagant nightmares surged through me with colossal force, and I immediately felt fully reconciled to an America capable of producing such violent yet mannered prose and horror that was so delicately expressed. People certainly did not suffer from boredom there. My imagination was fired, not that I consisted of much more than imagination and sensibility. I learnt Poe's poetry by heart, I yearned for Ulalume, I walked in the cypress groves with Psyche, my soul's desire.

I remember these strange half-hallucinatory moments because I think that to some extent they have influenced me, yet they have also effaced all traces of more specific events from my memory. The only thing I can remember is that on 6 September 1919, Anne, Sarah and a few friends got together to celebrate my birthday. There were cakes and everyone congratulated me. At that age I did not require much more to make me feel happy. My cousin described the marvellous colours of the South which reminded me of mother's stories. So I was going to see all that! I laughed and made silly jokes.

The day came when I had to think about what luggage I would take. My father decided that it was useless to buy a trunk and that one of his large suitcases would be sufficient. I knew these suitcases well. They were ones he brought back from his trips and each time they would bear some new label in a language that was often incomprehensible. Even empty, these suitcases were heavy, for they were made of the thickest leather. I filled mine with a few shirts and lots of books.

Departure was a terrible wrench for me. Up until then, I had not believed it would really happen, since nothing was ever totally true. Nevertheless, the day came when I had to walk down the Rue de la Pompe to look for a taxi and all the way along the street I wondered whether I would let myself down by crying. My cousin, who never ever wanted to go back home, looked as glum as I did about the future. In spite of that, we found ourselves at the Gare de Lyon soon enough and, in due course, on the train to Marseilles. Sarah stretched out in her seat and fell asleep in sorrow while I gloomily watched the landscape around Fontaine-bleau which suddenly seemed to provide pleasant memories. In my mind I clung desperately to the name of each station that we passed.

There are things I forget. Does one deliberately forget certain things as many psychiatrists suggest? In any case, I do remember that several weeks before my departure my father sent me to the United States Embassy to procure my passport. At that time the passport office was situated on the small square that lies to one side of the Galliera Museum. Unless I am mistaken, a statue of Rochambeau stood in the middle of a terreplein surrounded by plane trees. I can still see all that in my mind's eye, as well as the grocer's shop which formed the corner with the Rue Pierre-Charron. I can also see, and this is what prevented me from entering the building to which I had been directed rather more boldly, an American soldier on duty outside, who was much taller than me and much better looking. This decorative creature must have been very well cared for, since his khaki uniform was tailored to perfection and embellished with white gaiters which struck me as extra-ordinarily elegant. Under the peak of his cap, which reached down almost to his nose, could be seen, if one dared to look, a face with perfect features that reminded one of the curly-headed gods of Greek art.

I felt so overcome with confusion that I walked round to the far side of Rochambeau's statue, then I went to look in the window of the grocer's shop, and then I sat down on a bench in the square and pulled a book out of my pocket, although I could not read a line. There was nothing for it but to cross the square, stride past the magnificent fellow on sentry duty and dive in like a rat into a hole. That is the way I saw things. I felt insignificant, in fact, and even rather ridiculous alongside this young man who seemed to come from a different world to mine, yet I could not help staring at him. 'If they're all like him over there . . . ', I thought to myself. I wondered why I was not as good looking or strong as he was. The memory that remains of those moments is one of unaccountable suffering. At last, ashamed of being so feeble, I walked across the square and straight past the soldier.

'Hey there!'

I stopped dead as if I had been changed to stone, and the young man asked me what I was doing and who had I come to see. In a voice that was hoarse and slightly aggressive, as the voices of those who are shy often are, I explained that I was American and that I wanted a passport.

'Okay', he said. 'It's at the end on the left.'

He turned away from me and whistled as he once again began to pace up and down outside the entrance.

I saw him once again, for having made my request that day, I had to come back a few days later, and this time he looked even more handsome. I returned home in a mood of deep melancholy. Certainly, before seeing him I had not been aware that a single human being could accommodate so much grace and physical perfection, and I continued to be astonished by the mystery. How did one dare speak to him? What must his life be like? For weeks the image of him burned inside me. To tell the truth, it has never really left me, and I was to find aspects of it, in one form or another, throughout the whole of my work.

Since I am on the subject of memories which one subconsciously avoids mentioning, either out of modesty or out of innate caution, I have remembered something else from much further back, which I ought to put in its correct place: about 1913 or 1914. Among the enormous art books in my parents' library, which were so thickly bound that one had to carry them in both arms and only open them on the large table in the dining-room, or on the drawing-room carpet, there was one with a photograph of a remarkable painting. In it, could be seen a Roman woman at her toilette, surrounded by women who were nobly attired in pleated robes, and who attended her and perfumed her body. There was a door at the back of the room, however, which opened and a young slave-girl drew back a curtain to announce something such as: 'Madam is served' or 'Your lord has just slit his veins', and not only was this slave-girl extremely beautiful but she was also completely naked. No shadow disturbed the dark skin of her body and there was no trace of her sex either. That is what I noted so admiringly. She was beautiful and yet there was nothing distinctive on the front of her body. I beheld the image of an ideal being, beautiful, slender and totally asexual. I desired this creature, and I desired her so much that I thought I must be committing a sin and so I turned over the page. I wanted mankind in its entirety, both male and female, to be like the little slave-girl, but one ought not to look at naked bodies, and so with a heavy heart I closed the book shut, although I returned several times afterwards to take another look.

From this point onwards I no longer need to rely solely on my memory. There is an abundance of documents. Almost everything that I wrote at this time and up until 1922 has been preserved, in spite of moving house, the war, and all those circumstances that can lead to papers being lost or burned.

On the morning of 19 September 1919, I found myself on board the ship that was to take us from Marseilles to Naples, where members of the American Red Cross in Italy were due to embark. I was surrounded by Americans, and still more Americans! In the joyful commotion of voices there were accents from every part of America, dominated by the twang of the North, the Yankee accent which I could not get used to and which quite upset me at the time. Yet I was very aware of the general good humour all around me. It seemed to me that all people did was enter and leave cabins, laughing and shouting. I had remained inside mine, prey to the gloomiest thoughts, for it broke my heart to be leaving France, when a young American officer rushed in and yelled:

'You idiot, what are you doing there dreaming? Get up on deck with your passport!'

We did not leave until the late morning. I underwent all the necessary formalities and afterwards I began to wander from deck to deck like a convict in a prison yard. At this point something occurred which left a particular impression on me. I was on the lower deck where all the baggage was piled up when two young sailors, both members of the crew, came up to me. I talked to them with such pleasure, almost effusively, for in my mind they might be the last Frenchmen I would ever speak to. In fact this departure seemed to me rather like the end of life itself.

I no longer recall what the sailors said to me, but they took me to a narrow staircase which led down to the holds. I can see clearly the little door which opened onto what seemed to be a vast cavern. Another sailor, perhaps slightly older, was there and close to him was a fourth person, a girl I thought, whom I did not notice at first because she was so small. It was a cabin boy with reddish blond hair and he smiled up at me . . . I turned away quickly and climbed back up to the top deck.

This very mysterious little scene left an indelible mark on me precisely because I did not understand it, but I often thought about it afterwards.

My cousin Sarah had already got to know everybody, particularly those among what she considered to be the fair sex, and it looked as if it would be a happy crossing for everyone except for the writer of these lines.

I tried to dredge up from deep within me some enthusiasm for the idea that I was leaving for America, but one might as well have attempted to light a damp firework. I was so shy I hardly spoke to anybody except to my cousin when she was able to spare me a couple of minutes of her time which she always did very graciously:

'You're not sociable enough', she told me, 'you should come out of your shell and speak to one or two people. I am sure that you would be very popular.'

Those were the very words she used. The poor girl could not know what a sad death awaited her . . . As we steamed away from port, she stood close to me and said: 'Oh France, France, we will see her again one day.' She was never to see her again, for she was to die in hospital, six years later, just at the moment she had planned to return to Paris.

In the morning, two days later, I woke early, roused from sleep by the quietness of the engines, and I looked out of the porthole. It was one of the most marvellous moments of my youth. 'Naples!' I shouted. We were in the bay and Vesuvius stood out pink in the rising sun. I think only Italy has ever given me a feeling of earthly happiness that surpassed all expectation. Why should that be? I cannot say, but seeing that golden light, those thousands of multi-coloured houses, that blue sea under a blue sky, I was suddenly overcome with a sense of total joy which made me do some very strange things.

We were told that we were free to spend the whole day ashore at our leisure. Small groups were organized, but I decided to spend the day on my own. I did not want to share the pleasure of discovering Naples with people whom I secretly considered to be barbarians, for I was already withdrawing into myself, erecting those wretched walls around me that were to cause me so much suffering in America. Naples should be for me alone.

In order to go ashore, it was necessary to descend a metal gangway that had been hung alongside the ship and board one of the small launches that were moored there for this purpose. I don't know why, but I was the last to disembark. It was probably because I wanted to be sure that I should be alone, and in fact I was the only American on that particular launch. I was not alone, however. There was a man who rowed and, sitting opposite me, a young boy. Had I any cigarettes? No, I had none. With my boater perched like a halo on my head, I gazed at the landscape with an exhilarated but, I am sure, satisfied and stupid expression while the man and the young boy conversed in a language I did not know, the Neapolitan dialect. After a while, the boy began to address me in Italian. First, there were compliments. You speak well for a *straniero*. We had almost reached land. I was already on my feet, ready to jump ashore, when he suggested that I might like to *far l'amore* with his sister who, he told me, was a very beautiful girl. I shook my head. He began to laugh. If I was not interested in the girl, perhaps he could take her place? I did not understand what he meant and blushed. By this time I was on the quayside, pulling a few lire from my pocket which I gave to the boatman and hurrying towards the stone steps which led up to the port, but all along the way I could not help hearing the shrill voice of the disappointed boy and what he was saying, to judge by the tone, was far from polite. It was a mixture of Italian and Neapolitan. I made out the expression *va morir ammazzato* (go and get beaten to death) which I knew because I had heard it in Genoa, but there must have been many more highly colourful remarks which escaped me. Once again, I felt strangely unsettled, yet a minute later I was sitting in a cab, a *carrozzella*, and asking the driver to take me to the Museo Nazionale.

Why? Only now do I ask myself this question. At first, it seems entirely natural that I should want to see one of the finest museums in Europe, but who had told me about it? No one. I knew there was a museum there and I was very keen on museums. Nevertheless, I cannot help feeling that there was something altogether less straightforward about this, and much more mysterious than a mere tourist's curiosity. A sort of rendezvous had been contrived. I shall mention this again later.

As I sat in my *carrozzella*, my arms stretched wide over the top of the seat, I looked out over one of the dirtiest but most marvellous cities in the world. 'To live here', I thought, 'Oh! how wonderful to live here.' When we reached the doors of the museum, I was swindled by the *vetturino*, which seemed quite normal to me so I gave him what he wanted without arguing, and I entered the building which, if I remember correctly, was red.

What amazes me today is how little life's minor events taught me anything about myself. Either I could not, or did not wish to be told anything, and I stubbornly resisted heeding any useful advice.

I was much more deeply troubled by matters of the flesh than I realized, and there was something within me that insisted on hiding this fact from me. What shall I call this something? I don't know, but I would not be entirely honest if I did not admit that it had been a cause of much misery. Why not put it more simply and say that the whole question has tortured me? It tortured me because I knew only too well that our life after death is only the extension of our life in this world, and that he who directs himself towards God on earth will live for ever with God in Heaven; that he who has rejected God in this life may not find Him on the other side of the tomb. Intuitively, I knew all that in 1919 and I knew it when I walked across the ground-floor rooms of the national museum in Naples, for I moved through them as if I were being led.

When I was in the room with the Pompeian bronze sculptures, my blood began to pump through my body with such force that I had to stand still. Can I ever forget the moment? The room was empty. Set against the walls were glass cabinets full of small objects and all around me were bronze statues of every size. They took my breath away. I realized I was in the very heart of what was for me a forbidden region. The entire spiritual part of me was urging me to leave this dangerous place but I remained transfixed. It is not enough to say that nakedness flaunted itself within these walls: voluptuousness triumphed in all its myriad forms. At first, I did not dare to fix my gaze on anything in particular, but gradually, the longer I stayed, I felt strangely reassured. Was I not in a museum which everybody came to see to admire its work of art? The expression 'works of art' covered everything, and justified everything too. I was doing nothing wrong and I would not mind telling anyone what I had done that morning.

I approached one statue and then another with a certain respect, spending more time at first looking at those that interested me the least. I did this out of a strange need to deceive my conscience, to recompense it in some way — as if one could — and to stifle its protests before I reached the particular statue that I had noticed from a distance.

It shocked me. That is not too strong a word. At first I found there was something appalling about it, and then, in a way I cannot describe, I was seduced by it. Some would find it inoffensive; it could be placed before a drawing class and innocently copied by fifty or more pupils, yet it possessed a terrifying power of corruption for those who could see. In a state of delight mixed with horror, I paced around this truly infernal statue. If ever a man were bewitched in this life, I was. How long did I stay there? I really don't know. Time no longer existed; I gradually felt myself becoming someone else, someone whose eyes had been opened, who had been enlightened.

There must have been other visitors in the room, but I was not aware of them. Neither was I aware that I was being watched by a warden who eventually approached me quietly. A strange scene followed. When I saw this man standing close to me, I knew for certain that he had been observing me for some time. I cannot recall his features, but he was clearly older than me even though he must still have been a young man. I remember how politely he introduced the merest suggestion of complicity. He greeted me and asked what the *signorino* thought of the statue. *Bellissima, no?*

I felt embarrassed, but the janitor's smile reassured me. Once again I was reassured by something I did not understand, but what had I understood? Suddenly the statue no longer struck me as at all indecent, but rather graceful and wonderfully beautiful, and another thing that made me feel less anxious was the fact that the male attributes were reduced to the minimum and were no more than the very stylized and idealized image of a part of the body that horrified me. Before my eyes was some sort of beautiful monster that did not correspond to any known reality, child, man or woman, yet which somehow had taken on aspects of what was most seductive in all three of them, and which might have come out of Baudelaire's dream. It is true, I could have ignored the janitor's question and pretended that I did not understand. In actual fact, I murmured: '*Bellissima.*'

He explained the statue's provenance and told me that it was attributed to a famous sculptor. Pink with confusion, I listened to him and, as I began to relax, I made a few remarks which I have forgotten, but he congratulated me on my Italian before returning to the subject of the statue. How benevolently this man looked at me as he spoke! I have not forgotten his warm, almost caressing voice and his smiling eyes, even though I can no longer recall his precise features. I only have an impression of him, but it is a very powerful one. Eventually, he asked me whether I would like to own a replica of the statue, a copy that was so good that you could not tell them apart. Oh! yes. Certainly. But surely that wasn't possible? Entirely possible, *signorino*. But I was on my way to America. . . Very well, it would be sent to America if I would kindly leave my address. And . . . how much would that be? A very small amount: one hundred and fifty lire. The price seemed a trifle. I gave the money and my address to the janitor who flashed a smile and assured me that I would have the statue for Christmas. And could I just have one more look before I left. . . He pointed to a bench: '*Si accomodi!*' After that he left me on my own.

Now, of all the encounters I have ever had on this earth, my meeting with this man was certainly the most sinister. I do not mean to insinuate that I had actually met the devil himself! The janitor cannot be blamed for certain things which I shall relate in another volume, but there can be no doubt that if he had not been there, the course of my life might have been different.

As I left the museum, I began to suspect that I had been very naïve to believe that I could have bought a copy of the statue for such a small sum of money. Had I not been told a hundred times to beware of Neapolitans? This one, however, had been particularly kind and, I have to admit, very charming. But why? That is what I could not work out. I would soon see, before Christmas, whether or not he had made a fool of me.

While I was looking around the castle of the Angevin kings which the Neapolitans call *il maschio angovino*, I met my cousin and a group of her friends who invited me to lunch, and it was arranged that we should all go to Pompeii in the afternoon.

Here again my memory refuses to provide me with the answers I need, although I can suddenly see myself in the streets of the dead city. We were walking from house to house, from ruin to ruin, and here we are at last at the place everyone has been waiting to see, the street of the brothels. Move to one side, ladies, and kindly be patient enough to wait here for a moment. . . We men are going inside what remains of one of these houses. On the wall you can make out marks carved into the stone to indicate the number of clients? 'That is the way they kept their accounts. . .' This phrase has remained in my mind, but what happened next even more so, for the guide drew open the shutters and showed us some frescoes which most of us looked at with a mixture of embarrassment and delight. In my case, along with strong curiosity, I experienced feelings of fear and repugnance. Albano was a mere novice compared to the perpetrator of these cynical and violent paintings. There were horrifying anatomical details — I nevertheless looked at them, and I looked at them very carefully, but inwardly they revolted me. I did not dare look at the reactions of the rest of the party. In any case, they kept quiet despite the coarse and mocking banter of our guide, who then proceeded to offer us a complete series of reproductions of the most salacious of the frescoes for about two lire. To show that I was a man, and to do as everyone else did, I also gave my two lire and received in exchange six or eight ghastly little photographs, several of which depicted positions which seemed to me to be inexplicable. Now the ladies are waiting for us, *signori*. Don't forget the guide!

We left Naples that same evening having taken aboard, together with a dozen Americans, a rather unprepossessing old English lady. I forget what her reasons for going to the United States were, if I ever knew them, but she was taking the opportunity of a berth in this Red Cross ship which took a few other passengers as well. In any case, she disappeared into her cabin and only emerged again two days later.

I awoke the next morning in the port of Palermo where we were to spend the whole of that day. We were given leave to go ashore and do as we wished, provided that everyone was on board again by sunset. This voyage was rather like a cruise. Everyone was good-humoured and they formed themselves into small groups to visit the town's attractions. The name of Monreale was on everyone's lips. It was Monreale that one had to see, they said. So, en route it was for Monreale.

With my usual unsociability, I decided I would not go to Monreale with the barbarians. That is what I called them then. Dear barbarians without a drop of malice in their hearts, I should like to know in what way I was superior to them, but let us not go into that. So I walked around the town of Palermo on my own with a book under my arm. Which book was it? The poetry of Edgar Allan Poe which I had bought at Galignani's a week ago. I must have seemed very pretentious, but I would have been amazed if anyone had suggested as much, for I always had a book under my arm.

After wandering here and there, I found myself in a magical place which I shall never forget. I walked around the deserted gardens of San Giovanni-degli-Eremiti like a man who dreams he has discovered a paradise on earth. Above me, the domed cupolas of the small cloister shone like oranges cut in half against a deep blue sky, and beneath the trees with their intoxicating perfumes there was a wonderful coolness. I sat down on a stone bench and dreamt I was a monk in some bygone age. All around me were flowers whose scents and colours so entranced me that, provided it were painless, I think I would happily have died there among the delights of that solitude. No one could see me. I really was alone. I opened my book at my favourite poem and, as if possessed, I whispered:

> . . . *of cypress with Psyche my soul*. . .

As these wonderful scents wafted over me, I had the feeling

that I was being transported to the heart of some unknown world where there was no suffering. Here, in a strange way, I rediscovered religion in its most seductive guise and, I should also say, in its most illusory one, for at the time I confused religion with an innocent, but pagan, sensuality. I was searching for happiness. The memory of those bronze idols that I had lingered over only twenty-four hours earlier was far away now! I had an amazing facility for forgetting what had previously so totally captivated me. In the joy of that transient moment I was filled with such pleasure that I laughed out aloud.

After a long pause, I picked a leaf of mint which I placed between the pages of my book. I tried to imagine that the book was a priest's breviary and that I was wearing a habit. Under my breath, I sang the hymns that I had heard in the chapel of the Rue Cortambert. . . But I could not stay there. Wherever you are, whenever you are happy, you always have to leave.

On the ship, I came across the barbarians again. They had been drinking a variety of wines and, like children, were all speaking at once. Laden with souvenirs, they bustled each other along the corridors, laughing and shouting like schoolchildren on holiday.

'You should have come', my cousin called out. 'Monreale. . .'

She went off and then reappeared. 'Oh! Don't look quite so solemn!'

Once more she went away to join a group of friends who were cackling away happily and showing off their multi-coloured scarves.

That evening I dined tête-à-tête with the English lady. To tell the truth, they did not know at which table they should put me, because I was not what was known as a 'good mixer', in other words, a jolly and sociable person. I was shy and serious, and I must have been rather boring. That is probably why they thought it sensible to seat me at the same table as the new passenger. She was a lady of a certain age, who reminded me of Mouser, for in spite of the granite-like severity of her countenance one could see from the way she dressed that she was clearly fond of frills, yet no amount of the ribbons or jewels with which she bedecked herself could sweeten her redoubtable physiognomy. She nevertheless did her best to be polite and gracious and she spoke to me with that curious mixture of kindliness and coldness that I have known in so many English people. I replied willingly to the questions she put to me, fairly indiscreetly too, for I was quite frank. She raised her eyebrows once or twice, and as we were cutting our fruit, she suddenly laid down her knife and came out with this expression which I have never forgotten because she said it in a rather reproachful way:

'You are a dreamer and a poet.'

'*You are a dreamer and a poet.*' I have often thought of these words and wondered whether she intended them as a compliment or a rebuke. I did not answer her, but something inside me replied: 'Yes'.

We drifted towards Spain under a radiant sky, and throughout the pleasures of the one big party which was what our voyage really was, I kept well away from all the amorous intrigues which meant nothing to me. There was one young woman, however, whose company I would willingly have sought if I had had a chance. Unfortunately, most of the boys had the same idea and she was always snatched from me. The lady in question was a Miss Lamar, an extremely pretty girl from New Orleans who, from the very first day had been friendly towards me. To tell the truth, she was a good twelve years older than me and for some reason she seemed to have taken it into her head to round off my education. She was dark-haired, slender and extremely elegant, and sitting on deck one day she pointed to an empty deckchair next to hers. I stretched out on it without any embarrassment for the simple reason that Miss Lamar was a brunette and not blonde. According to my views at the time, beauty was always blond, and only beauty could intimidate. Nevertheless, Miss Lamar was most charming and her skin reminded me of that of Marceline*, the girl who I had once adored so long ago. She made a few complimentary remarks, one or two of which I remember. She told me, for example, that I did not speak like someone from the North, which pleased me. In fact, she and I were compatriots. Then she told me that if it ever occurred to me to settle in New Orleans, I could speak French from morning till night and I would be understood by many of the delightful inhabitants. She dropped these remarks casually as she gazed out over the Mediterranean and they found an echo within me for I dreamed of such a place. Miss Lamar stroked the invisible creases of the silk scarf she wore around her neck. I liked being with her and I soon became accustomed to paying her regular visits. Very gradually, she made me feel more and more at ease with her, but there was always a moment when another, braver boy would come and sit down on the other side of her, and suddenly it was as if I no longer existed. Declarations of love were scribbled on visiting cards which were pinned to

* See *The Green Paradise*

her cabin door. I believe she must have had a fairly ardent temperament. One afternoon she had the strange notion of discussing religion with me and asked me how someone 'as intelligent as you' could believe in the infallibility of the Pope. I looked at her as if she had played a dirty trick on me, then I replied that Cardinal Newman had certainly believed in it. Why Cardinal Newman? Well, the only other Catholic author I knew was Pascal. She fluttered her eyelids. She was obviously not prepared for Cardinal Newman and there we left the matter.

Two days later, we reached the Spanish coast at Almería. Once again we were free to go ashore and walk around until the evening. Once again I wandered off on my own. I climbed to the top of a tower and was blinded by the whiteness of the town spread out below me. Spain, I thought, you are in Spain. But no one had ever heard of Almería. I tried to imagine what my life might have been like in a place like this before the heat of the sun drove me down from the tower and into the streets where the cool shade was as refreshing as water. I bought a tambourine and castanets in a shop. Why? Because long ago there had been similar ones in my sister Eleanore's room in the Rue de Passy.

Back on board ship, I met my travelling companions who were worn out by a day spent sightseeing and buying much more extravagant presents than mine. They all wanted to be Spaniards: the sound of castanets and tambourines echoed out of every cabin and the red and yellow colours of Spain were suddenly all the rage.

At dinner, I was surprised to find myself sitting next to a young married couple, both from Almería, who were leaving to settle in the United States. Everyone thought them very good looking and, each in their own particular way, they certainly were, although they were also rather solemn, as the Spanish can sometimes be. Because of this, it had been decided that they would not be 'good mixers', which was why they were put at the same table as the English lady and me. Nothing remarkable happened at our first meal together. No one said a word. Albion looked on from afar and I only managed the occasional furtive glance at our new companions. With his inky black hair and his large gloomy eyes, the husband only struck me as being handsome in a very conventional way, whereas his wife was of a much rarer and more delicate breed. Under her half-closed eyelids could be seen pupils of a blue that would sometimes appear grey and sometimes violet, and her small face was framed by pale gold hair. She bowed her head so gracefully. By comparison with her, her husband looked as strong as a stag, square-shouldered, solid and serious. He was clearly not a man to meddle with, but he was polite and at the end of dinner he gave us a wave which I tried to return as best I could and which the Englishwoman did not even notice. She wore the indignant look of someone who has been made to eat at the zoo. I could foresee a succession of rather gloomy lunches and dinners.

Miss Lamar was curious to know how we had got on with the new arrivals, so the next morning I sat beside her, basking in her favour, for she was kind enough to dismiss her other admirers in order to retain my company. I no longer remember what it was I said to her, but it pleased me to see her smile, and she would smile frequently at me.

I think the moment has come to admit to something which rather reveals my vanity and which I have avoided mentioning. One day when we were crossing the Mediterranean from Sicily to Spain, I was sitting beside Miss Lamar when she remarked that men had extremely large feet. Now, since I was stretched out on a deckchair, it was hard to conceal my own feet which suddenly appeared immense to me, and although I don't believe they are any bigger than normal, I took Miss Lamar's comments to heart. Accordingly, the first thing I did when we arrived in Almería was to go around the town's shoe shops to look for a pair that were smaller than the size I usually wore. I did better than I could have hoped, and that evening I returned on board wearing a small pair of purple leather shoes. By stepping carefully and as little as possible on tiptoes, I managed to disguise the pain I felt as I walked around the ship. Taking them off that evening was such blissful relief. I walked on deck next morning, my flesh crushed by what I thought of as my Spanish hobnailed boots, but there could be little doubt that my feet looked small. One morning when I was sitting next to Miss Lamar she gave a delicate smile and said simply:

'New shoes'. And she added: 'Very nice'.

I thanked her.

'Are they Spanish?'

'How did you guess?'

'Oh! By the colour', she said.

And by the dolour, I muttered to myself. Yet there's a certain pleasure in suffering.

That evening there was a small drama. I was strolling up and down the deck when suddenly, to my great surprise, the shoes felt comfortable for the first time. At last! My feet have got used to them, I thought to myself. That was not the case at all and it only took a glance to realize what had actually happened. The fine purple leather had split, as if in protest, across the top of the shoe. I rushed back to my cabin and hurled my Spanish hobnailed boots out of the

~ 202 ~

porthole and into the Atlantic. If one looked carefully I dare say they could still be found.

To return to the young married couple from Almería, I began to get used to them and soon the three of us were laughing together for, however much they tried to be serious, they were scarcely older than me and in some ways just as childish. Beneath what they considered to be obligatory gravity, there was an exuberant zest which I think must have shocked the Englishwoman. Yet she, too, was human and occasionally she would smile, although she considered that I was wrong to joke quite so much. Eventually I became very friendly with the Spaniards and it was clear that the feeling was mutual.

Now they had also made friends with another young man on board. I can no longer visualize his face. He was American and I remember that he was Catholic, even rather excessively so. We had more than one conversation about the Church and he maintained that the French had scarcely any faith by comparison with the Spanish. According to him, one only had to see the manner in which Parisians attended Mass, the casual way in which they came and went as they pleased, the lack of respect that men showed when they remained standing at the consecration, and how few went to communion (that was true at the time), whereas in Spain. . . He could often be seen chatting to the couple from Almería and one evening as I was walking past, he said to them:

'You should show Julian the lovely things you are taking to America, for Julian is mad about things like that. . .' (I have remembered this rather silly phrase.)

There was a slight hesitation as they wondered whether

they should allow me into their cabin, then with a laugh they agreed. 'Yes, if you would like to.'

Feeling slightly embarrassed, I was taken to the young couple's cabin and, very charmingly, they opened their suitcases to show me what I think were various kinds of lace after which, having exchanged a few pleasantries, I reckoned it was time to leave. The American boy was with me and when we were on deck he made some remarks which I would find hard to forget.

'Wouldn't you like to be hidden in their cabin at this moment, watching them?'

'Watching them!' I exclaimed.

'Oh!' my friend continued, 'Surely you can imagine how their bodies must entwine, how he undresses her. . .'

'But they're not doing anything wrong.'

'No, because they are married. They can do what they want. But it would be nice to watch.'

I looked at him in amazement. In my own mind, conjugal relations between married people were extremely rare. Where did that notion come from? I really don't know, but I used to think that once was enough to conceive a human being, and that these entwinings that the American spoke of, were superfluous, if not reprehensible. My ignorance about these matters was such that even a nun might have ticked me off. What shocked me even more was that my friend asked me a little later if I would be going to communion next Sunday. Mass was said on board ship, and I think I did take communion with the American and the Spanish couple for we were the only Catholics on board, but I still considered the remarks he had made about the young married couple no less shocking.

Eight or ten times a day while we were still in the

Mediterranean, everybody would rush over to one side of the ship or the other whenever anything new could be seen on the horizon. It was usually only the distant smoke from the funnel of another vessel, or else some dolphins playing close by which would provoke child-like admiration. Personally, I grew tired of all this. The thought that with every minute I was travelling a little further away from France made me feel very gloomy and I remained on my own as much as possible. One morning when we were all having breakfast, there was a sudden hubbub of voices and within a few seconds the dining-room was virtually empty. More dolphins or a passing ship, I thought, and since I could not be bothered to go up on deck I remained seated and finished my breakfast in peace. A little time went by, then there was a great commotion and everyone came downstairs again.

'Did you see it?' asked my cousin as she walked by.

'See what?'

'The Rock of Gibraltar of course!'

I had passed the Rock of Gibraltar without seeing it. In my state of mind at the time it did not matter to me at all.

Twenty years later, I would actually stay there. It was in December 1939. I was returning from America where I had been living for several months, and the war had brought me back to Europe. Our ship, the *Excalibur*, was required to dock at Gibraltar for a period of three weeks and I doubt if there was a single part of the Rock that I did not get to know. Ah well! So you didn't learn your lesson in 1919? Very well, you'll have to wait until 1939 and in much more melancholy circumstances. . . In such ways does life take us to task.

While the sun shone on us in the Mediterranean, the weather in the Atlantic was gloomy. With my habit of seeing images of the world whose significance was sometimes clear and sometimes obscure, I often wondered what this long crossing could signify, and eventually I convinced myself that it was all taking place in the invisible regions of the mind, a vast, laborious transition from one mental landscape to another. The land of my childhood was being taken from me. That was all there was to it. Beyond the thousands of waves which seemed to dance furiously beneath the grey skies, there, surely, lay the dour lands of adulthood.

I remember that there was a young American on board who was built like a beanpole, but whose head was perfectly normal and unremarkable. He looked like a Greek god wearing a cap. Why should I remember that he was reading Zola's *La Terre*? I remember because one afternoon he was leaning over the ship's rails with this book, which had a yellow cover, in his hands. He read out a passage which rather disturbed me and then, with a gesture which I shall never forget, he hurled the novel into the sea. 'Filth', he yelled.

Something had changed within me of late. I no longer felt exactly the same person I was when I left, and the day came when I took out of my wallet the photographs I had bought in Pompeii, and I did as the young American had done and let them float away on the Atlantic. Some qualms of conscience probably drove me to this gesture, but the truth is always a little more modest than one thinks, at least when told in its entirety; I was also frightened of being searched by the customs in New York. I was equally ashamed of being a boy who carried around dirty pictures in his pockets, because this did not fit with the image I had of myself, and the fear of separation from God was suddenly stronger than ever. Those invisible walls that had been built around me in childhood were holding firm.

The horizon was sometimes hidden by mist. It seemed to me that as we approached America everything was becoming more harsh: the ocean was darker, the light was colder, and something or someone seemed to be coming towards me. Was it a premonition? But then what was the use of premonitions? How could I know that one of the most violent religious crises of my life was about to tear me apart in a few weeks time and that the suffering that would await me was of a kind I had never experienced? I became anxious and restless, and I had the impression that on board no one was laughing as much, that the holidays were over. Then one morning, as if in a mirage, I saw in the distance a city rise out of the water; it had the whiteness of a dream, clear, sharp and cold under a cloudless sky, and my heart began to beat with hope.